A Burning Light

The Life and Ministry
of John the Baptist

Robert J. Matthews

Published and Distributed by:

PUBLISHING & DISTRIBUTION

Granite Publishing and Distribution, L.L.C.
868 North 1430 West • Orem, UT 84057
(801) 229-9023 • Toll Free (800) 574-5779
FAX (801) 229-1924

Cover Artwork: "John the Baptist Preaching" by Del Parson
© by Intellectual Reserve, Inc.
Used by Permission

Cover Design by: Tamara Ingram

Library of Congress Catalog Card Number: 00-105996
ISBN: 1-890558-94-X

Contents

Preface

John the Baptist is unique among men. The world does not understand him, and even members of the Church frequently do not appreciate him. A large bronze statue of John the Baptist on Temple Square in Salt Lake City and another at the banks of the Susquehanna River near Harmony, Pennsylvania, attest to the special place that he holds in the history and theology of The Church of Jesus Christ of Latter-day Saints. Yet in many instances individuals in the Church are not familiar enough with the numerous events of his ministry to comprehend even a measure of his greatness.

I have written this study with the hope that it might cultivate a wider knowledge and a greater appreciation for the life and work of this great forerunner and witness of the Savior than is commonly enjoyed. The scope of the work encompasses that information which is given in the ancient and modern scriptures, as well as in the teachings of Joseph Smith and other latter-day prophets. The point of view is that of an increased awareness of John's ministry in three dispensations of the gospel, in the light of latter-day revelation, which gives a fuller view and a more complete knowledge than can be obtained from the Bible alone.

With the recent discovery and translation of ancient scrolls found near the Dead Sea, new interest in John the Baptist has been kindled in the world of biblical scholarship, and numerous books and articles have been written in the past two decades by non-LDS scholars in an attempt to clarify John's mission and to link him with the people of the scrolls. However, most of what has been written on this theme is speculative. The value of the scrolls, as they pertain to John the Baptist, is found not so much in the information they give concerning him, but in the *interest* that they have kindled about him.

It is worthy of note that the standard works of the Church — the Bible, the Book of Mormon, the Doctrine and Covenants, and the Pearl of Great Price — each contain significant information about the life, mission, and work of John the Baptist. Likewise, the Inspired Version of the Bible and the Prophet Joseph Smith's teachings offer a wealth of material about John and give many valuable insights. The availability of so much information, of which a considerable amount is found only in latter-day sources, invites a comprehensive study of John the Baptist, gathered from all of the sources, and written from the perspective of the gospel as it has been revealed in the present dispensation. Although there are a few books which deal with various phases of John's ministry from the point of view of latter-day revelation, such studies have been chiefly centered on other subjects and the connection with John is incidental. A separate study of the type described above has not yet been published, but this treatise is an attempt toward the accomplishment of such a task.

The basic source used in this study is the King James Version of the Bible. This is frequently supplemented by the "new translation" of the Bible made by the Prophet Joseph Smith and published under the title "Holy Scriptures, Inspired Version." I have examined the original manuscripts from which the Inspired Version was printed and am satisfied that the printed version is an accurate representation of the originals. All italics added for emphasis in scripture passages are mine.

Several other versions of the Bible are used to clarify some alternate marginal readings found in the King James Version. The most important of these are (1) the new Catholic Confraternity Edition (in English), copyright 1962; (2) *The Four Gospels According to the Eastern Version*, a 1933 English translation of ancient Syrian manuscripts by Dr. George M. Lamsa; (3) the American Standard Version of the Bible, printed in 1900; (4) The New English Bible, first printed in 1961; and (5) a German translation of the Bible published in Stuttgart in 1964, being a slight revision and modernization of Martin Luther's translation of the sixteenth century.

The reader will find some duplication and repetition in the chapters of this book, but this seemed necessary in order to permit a change of emphasis at different points and a plan of the book which is doctrinal and theological instead of simply biographical.

A word is perhaps needed about the dating system. I have made no attempt to offer exact dates; however, to give a sequence to the events, I have used a system corresponding with that usually offered by scholars, placing the birth of Jesus Christ at about 4 or 5 B.C. Some readers may object to this, and perhaps justly so, but this study follows rather closely the dating system used by J. Reuben Clark, Jr., in his book *Our Lord of the Gospels*. A more detailed explanation of this is given in the "Chronology of Events" preceding chapter one herein.

I have long held a fascination for the life of John the Baptist, and this interest alone has repaid me for the effort required to arrange the materials contained in this work.

Acknowledgments

This book was written over a period of three years, mostly during the night hours, and often in motel rooms or en route by air while traveling for the Department of Seminaries and Institutes of Religion. The idea of compiling a small book about John the Baptist, with particular emphasis on the information given in latter-day revelation and the teachings of the Prophet Joseph Smith, occurred to me several years ago. Since that time many people have expressed their interest and lent encouragement to the project. To all of these I owe a debt of appreciation. The book is intended to be serious, it is a private endeavor, and I alone am responsible for the contents and views. Particularly, I wish to thank my wife, Shirley, who patiently assisted throughout the entire time of writing and rewriting. To her and our three children, Camille, Dan, and Robbie, this work is affectionately dedicated.

Chronology of Events Associated with John the Baptist

The dates in this chronology are intended only as a guide to the sequence of events and are not purported to be exact either as to month or year. A dating system is used to correspond with the chronology of the life of Jesus employed by Pres. J. Reuben Clark, Jr., in *Our Lord of the Gospels*, which places the birth of Jesus Christ at about 4 B.C.* Bible references are from the King James Version, except where identified by "I.V.," signifying the Inspired Version by Joseph Smith. References from latter-day revelation are given in the usually accepted form.

---

*President Clark explained his use of this chronology:

"Some may sharply disagree with the computations (now accepted by many scholars) that fix the date of the Savior's birth at the end of 5 B.C., or the beginning or early part of 4 B.C. The Church has made no official declaration on the matter, beyond that contained in Verse 1 of Section 20 of the Doctrine and Covenants. In the early editions of the *Doctrine and Covenants Commentary* (by Brothers Hyrum M. Smith and Janne M. Sjodahl) this verse was interpreted as follows:

" 'The organization of the Church in the year 1830 is hardly to be regarded as giving divine authority to the commonly accepted calendar. There are reasons for believing that those who, a long time after our Savior's birth, tried to ascertain the correct time, erred in their calculations, and that the Nativity occurred four years before our era, or in the year of Rome 750. All that this Revelation means to say is that the Church was organized in the year that is commonly accepted as 1830, A.D.' (p. 138). Rome 750 is equivalent (say the scholars) to 4 B.C.

"This statement has been omitted in the latest edition of the *Commentary*.

"I am not proposing any date as the true date. But in order to be as helpful to

Approximate Date and Place	Event	Reference
B.C. 700 Jerusalem	Isaiah prophesies of a forerunner to prepare the way of the Lord.	Isa. 40:3
B.C. 600 Jerusalem	Lehi in vision sees a prophet preaching to the people and also baptizing the Messiah.	1 Ne. 10:7-10
B.C. 559-545 Western Hemisphere	Nephi speaks of the prophet who will prepare the way and baptize the Lamb of God.	1 Ne. 11:27 2 Ne. 31:4-8
B.C. 400 Jerusalem	Malachi prophesies of the messenger who would prepare the way before the Lord.	Mal. 3:1-3
B.C. 5, about January Jerusalem	Gabriel visits Zacharias and gives him a promise of a son. Elizabeth goes into retirement for about five months. Mary visits Elizabeth for about three months. During this time Zacharias is without the power of speech.	Luke 1:5-25, 39-56
B.C. 5, October Judea	John is born. The event is well known in the region round about. He is circumcised, named, ordained by an angel, and blessed by his father when he is eight days old. Later in his childhood he is baptized.	Luke 1:57-79 D&C 84: 24-28
B.C. 4, April Bethlehem	Jesus Christ is born.	Matt. 1:18-25 Luke 2:1-7
B.C. 4 Judea	Herod orders the slaughter of the children of Bethlehem. John is taken into the hill country by Elizabeth. Jesus is taken to Egypt. Zacharias dies about this time.	Matt. 2:16-18
B.C. 4-A.D. 26 Judea	John is in the desert areas of Judea until the time of his ministry.	Luke 1:80

[handwritten annotations: "Jul - Aug → Oct)" next to Mary visits; "30 YRS" next to B.C. 4-A.D. 26; "april is early in yr. (Roman not Jewish)" in bottom margin]

_____

students as I could, I have taken as the date of the Savior's birth the date now accepted by many scholars,—late 5 B.C., or early 4 B.C., because Bible Commentaries and the writings of scholars are frequently keyed upon that chronology and because I believe that so to do will facilitate and make easier the work of those studying the life and works of the Savior from sources using this accepted chronology" (*Our Lord of the Gospels* [Salt Lake City: Deseret Book Company, 1954], pp. vi-vii).

Approximate Date and Place	Event	Reference
A.D. 26, summer Judea	John's public ministry begins. He preaches to and baptizes many people. He encounters the Pharisees and Sadducees. He tells that the Messiah will come.	Matt. 3 Mark 1 Luke 3
A.D. 27, January to April Jordan River	Jesus comes from Nazareth in Galilee to the Jordan River to see John. John baptizes Jesus and sees the Holy Ghost descend upon Jesus. Jesus goes into the wilderness forty days to commune with God. Before baptizing Jesus, John has preached about six to nine months.	Matt. 3:15-17 Matt. 4:1-11
A.D. 27, April or May Bethabara beyond Jordan	John continues to preach and to baptize. To a delegation of priests and Levites sent to him by the Pharisees, John does not deny that he is an Elias to prepare the way, but insists that he is not the Christ or the Elias to restore all things. He testifies that Jesus is the Christ, the Lamb of God, and was among them although they didn't know him.	John 1:20-28, I.V.
A.D. 27, April or May Bethabara	On the next day John sees Jesus returning from the wilderness and identifies him as "the Lamb of God, which taketh away the sin of the world." He testifies that he knows by revelation that Jesus is the Son of God.	John 1:29-34
A.D. 27, April or May Bethabara	The next day, John sees Jesus again and identifies him as the Lamb of God to two of his (John's) disciples. They leave John and follow Jesus.	John 1:35-40 *andrew + John*
A.D. 27, summer Aenon near Salim. Judea?	John continues to preach and to baptize at Aenon near Salim.	John 3:23
A.D. 27, summer Aenon near Salim. Judea?	John bears his last recorded testimony of Christ. He tells his own disciples that Jesus will increase but he (John) must de-	John 3:23-36 John 4:1-2

Approximate Date and Place	Event	Reference
	crease, that Jesus is heavenly and John is earthly, and that they are to leave him and follow Jesus. Jesus and his disciples baptize even more people than John has done.	
A.D. 27, autumn Machaerus, east of the Dead Sea	John is imprisoned by Herod's order. Jesus leaves Judea immediately and takes his disciples through Samaria into Galilee. It has been about six to nine months since John baptized Jesus, and approximately eighteen months since John began his public ministry.	Matt. 4:12 Matt. 14:3-5 Mark 6:17-20 Luke 3:19-20 John 4:3-4, 43-44
A.D. 28, March Galilee	In Galilee John's disciples question Jesus about fasting. John is in prison near the Dead Sea at least 125 miles away. The event shows the extent of John's influence, for he has disciples even in Galilee, where he has apparently never been in person.	Matt. 9:14-17 Mark 2:18-22 Luke 5:33-39
A.D. 28, April Jerusalem	To the Jewish rulers in Jerusalem at the Passover, Jesus testifies of John as a "burning and a shining light." John is in prison at this time.	John 5:1, 33-35
A.D. 28, summer Galilee	John, while in prison, sends messengers to Jesus in Galilee. Jesus gives a great tribute to John.	Matt. 11:2-19 Luke 7:18-35
A.D. 28-29, winter? Machaerus	Jesus sends angels to John in prison.	Matt. 4:11, I.V.
A.D. 28-29, winter Machaerus	John is beheaded by order of Herod after about fourteen to eighteen months in prison. Jesus is in Galilee at the time, and Herod, hearing of Jesus soon afterward, thinks he is John risen from the dead. The twelve are on missions, having been sent forth two by two shortly before John's death. (John was killed after about 1½ years of his own	Matt. 14:6-11 Mark 6:21-28

Approximate Date and Place	Event	Reference
	ministry and about 1½ years before the death of Jesus.)	
A.D. 28-29, winter Place unknown, but probably near Machaerus	John's disciples bury his body in a tomb and come and tell Jesus in Galilee.	Matt. 14:10-12 Mark 6:25-29
A.D. 29, summer North of Galilee	The Transfiguration. Moses and Elijah appear to Jesus, Peter, James, and John. Jesus speaks of his own impending death and resurrection. John the Baptist's mission is a topic of discussion. John also seems to have been present at the Transfiguration.	Matt. 17:1-13 Mark 9:1-11, I.V. Luke 9:28-36
A.D. 30, April Jerusalem	Jesus asks the chief priests and elders of the Jews for a commitment about John's authority — whether it was earthly or divine. They hedge, and refuse to say. Thereupon Jesus declares to them that John came in righteousness and they ought to have believed him and repented, and that the preaching of John would stand against them in the day of judgment.	Matt. 21:23-32 Matt. 21:33-34, I.V.
A.D. 30 Place unknown	John is resurrected. Described as being "with Christ in his resurrection," he is possibly one of those of whom Matthew later writes as coming out of their graves and going into the Holy City after the resurrection.	D&C 133:55 Matt. 27:52-53
A.D. 1829, Friday, May 15 Near Harmony, Pennsylvania	John ministers to Joseph Smith and Oliver Cowdery and confers on them the Aaronic Priesthood by the laying on of hands.	Smith 2:68-72
Future	John is to drink the fruit of the vine with Jesus, in company with other prophets, at the Lord's second advent.	D&C 27:5-14

Handwritten annotations:
— did they ever transport bodies to (home town) in those days. (Even in winter?) Doubtful.
Bethlehem — miles fr Machaerus
Over 2 yrs since Jesus' bap.
— even tho John buried in Machaerus.--- So

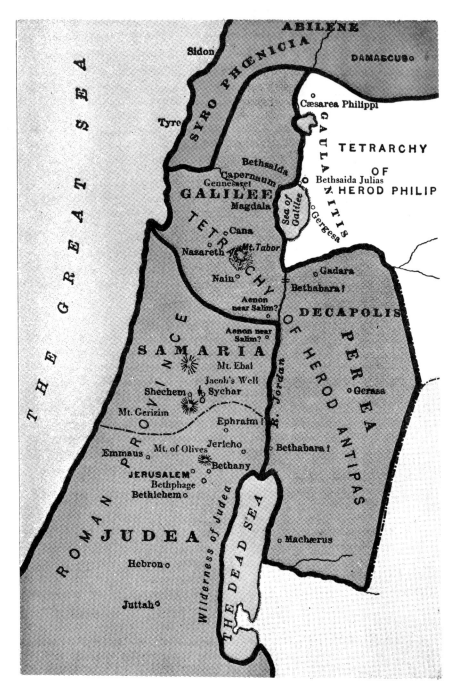

Palestine during the Ministry of John the Baptist

A Burning Light

1

John's Ministry Foretold

John the Baptist holds a special place in the history and the theology of The Church of Jesus Christ of Latter-day Saints. Most of us know two significant things about him: first, that he baptized Jesus; secondly, that he conferred the Aaronic Priesthood upon Joseph Smith and Oliver Cowdery on the banks of the Susquehanna River near Harmony, Pennsylvania. Although these are no doubt the two most important things about John, there is a great deal more that is interesting and thrilling about his life, character, and mission. He was considered an important enough character that his mission was made known to prophets and seers hundreds of years before his earthly advent. His birth was announced earlier by an angel and was accompanied by miraculous circumstances. He was emphatically and singularly eulogized by the Son of God himself.

But what other things might we learn of this prophet who — as a representative of the law of Moses, the baptizer of the Messiah in the meridian of time, and one of the heavenly messengers by whom the gospel was restored in modern times — was a prominent figure in three dispensations and is so specifically singled out in the scriptures of ancient and modern times? How much can we know about him? Who was he? What did he say? What did he do? What was his character? And what were the reactions of those who heard him preach?

There is no missing the fact that John the Baptist was one of the most divinely heralded and preannounced figures of history. Very few persons have been so singled out and categorized in advance by the sacred writings. Not only was his name specified beforehand by revelation, but much information about his activities, geographical location, and eating habits, and even the precise words and topics of his preaching were revealed to various prophets before his birth.

Ancient Prophecies

The earliest allusion to John the Baptist is found in Isaiah 40:3-5 (approximately 700 B.C.) as follows:

> The voice of him that crieth in the wilderness, Prepare ye the way of the Lord, make straight in the desert a highway for our God.
> Every valley shall be exalted, and every mountain and hill shall be made low: and the crooked shall be made straight, and the rough places plain:
> And the glory of the Lord shall be revealed, and all flesh shall see it together: for the mouth of the Lord hath spoken it.[1]

Matthew, Mark, and Luke each interpret this prophecy as having reference to John the Baptist: "For this is he that was spoken of by the Prophet Esaias [Isaiah]" (Matthew 3:1-3; also Mark 1:2-3; Luke 3:4-6). However, the book of John handles this passage a little differently, so that the Baptist himself is quoted as saying that he is the one of whom Isaiah spoke:

> Then said they unto him, Who are thou? . . .
> He [John] said, I am the voice of one crying in the wilderness, Make straight the way of the Lord, as said the prophet Esaias. [John 1:22-23.]

In Mark 1:2 it is inferred that Malachi also spoke of John the Baptist's mission. The passage, although not specifically identified by Mark, is actually found in Malachi 3:1, and therefore was written about 400 B.C. As quoted in Mark it reads:

> Behold, I send my messenger before thy face, which shall prepare thy way before thee.[2]

---

[1]This prophecy was not all fulfilled in the days of John the Baptist, nor have all of the provisions of it been fulfilled even now, but John's mission seems to have been the beginning of its fulfillment.

[2]In the King James Version, Old Testament quotations used in the New Testament are taken from a Greek translation known as the Septuagint (identified also as LXX), rather than from a Hebrew version of the Old Testament. For this reason these quotations often differ in spelling ("Esaias" is Isaiah) and in wording from the corresponding passage in the King James Old Testament, which is from a Hebrew text.

4

The allusion to Malachi 3:1 is obvious: "Behold, I will send my messenger, and he shall prepare the way before me."

The records of Matthew and Luke give a stronger affirmation that Malachi had reference to John the Baptist, for they handle the passage in such a way as to have Jesus himself declaring that John the Baptist was indeed the very one who Malachi had predicted would come. Said Jesus:

> For this is he, of whom it is written, Behold, I send my messenger before thy face, which shall prepare thy way before thee. [Matthew 11:10; also Luke 7:27.] [3]

In the Book of Mormon John the Baptist is not mentioned by name, but his mission is discussed with considerable detail in at least three instances. We quote first from father Lehi, who about 600 years before Christ spoke of John's mission:

> And he [Lehi] spake also concerning a prophet who should come before the Messiah, to prepare the way of the Lord —
> Yea, even he should go forth and cry in the wilderness: Prepare ye the way of the Lord, and make his paths straight; for there standeth one among you whom ye know not; and he is mightier than I, whose shoe's latchet I am not worthy to unloose. And much spake my father concerning this thing.
> And my father [Lehi] said he should baptize in Bethabara, beyond Jordan; and he also said he should baptize with water; even that he should baptize the Messiah with water.
> And after he had baptized the Messiah with water, he should behold and bear record that he had baptized the Lamb of God, who should take away the sins of the world. [1 Nephi 10:7-10.]

Lehi's declaration is similar to that given by Isaiah and Malachi, and even includes the identical thought, "Prepare ye the way of the Lord, and make his paths straight." But Lehi foretold these additional topics of John's preaching:

(1) "There standeth one among you whom ye know not."
(2) The Messiah "is mightier than I, whose shoe's latchet I am not worthy to unloose."

Lehi also stated that the prophet [John] would —

SPECIFIC PLACE!

(1) baptize with water in Bethabara beyond Jordan,
(2) baptize the Messiah with water, and
(3) afterward bear record that he had baptized the Lamb of God, who should take away the sins of the world.

---

[3] Again the text is that of the Septuagint rather than the Hebrew.

These words indicate that Lehi had an accurate foreknowledge concerning the activities, message, and geographical area of operation of John the Baptist.

Nephi also saw a similar vision of the work of John almost six hundred years before the time of John's mortal birth. Nephi's description of John's ministry is similar to that given by Lehi, but includes the additional fact that after Jesus was baptized the Holy Ghost descended upon him "in the form of a dove." Said Nephi:

> And I looked and beheld the Redeemer of the world, of whom my father had spoken; and I also beheld the prophet who should prepare the way before him. And the Lamb of God went forth and was baptized of him; and after he was baptized, I beheld the heavens open, and the Holy Ghost come down out of heaven and abide upon him in the form of a dove. [1 Nephi 11:27.]

Nephi later enlarged upon the subject:

> Wherefore, I would that ye should remember that I have spoken unto you concerning that prophet which the Lord showed unto me, that should baptize the Lamb of God, which should take away the sins of the world. . . .
>
> Wherefore, after he [Jesus] was baptized with water the Holy Ghost descended upon him in the form of a dove. [2 Nephi 31:4, 8.]

The reference to John as a forerunner to prepare the way for Jesus, to "make straight in the desert a highway for our God" (Isaiah 40:3), is an interesting allusion to the very ancient custom of sending forerunners immediately ahead of a royal chariot to clear the path of rocks and other obstacles. This practice is referred to in such places as 1 Samuel 8:11, 1 Kings 1:5, and Isaiah 62:10. Both Saul and Rehoboam kept "runners" for this purpose. Such forerunners would run ahead of the horse or carriage at a swift pace, shouting and proclaiming their leader, and using a staff if necessary to clear the way before the coming of the great one. Such is the picture of John the Baptist, given in the prophecies concerning him.

Announcement by the Angel Gabriel

A few months before John's birth into mortality, the angel Gabriel[4]

---

[4]The Prophet Joseph Smith has identified Gabriel as Noah (*Teachings of the Prophet Joseph Smith*, comp. Joseph Fielding Smith [Salt Lake City: Deseret Book Company, 1938], p. 157. Henceforth this work is cited simply as *Teachings*.). It is also understood that Noah is sometimes referred to as Elias (Joseph Fielding Smith, "Elias is Noah," *Answers to Gospel Questions*, 5 vols. [Salt Lake City: Deseret Book Company, 1957-66], 3:138-41).

came to Zacharias and announced that the latter would become the father of a son:

> . . . Fear not, Zacharias: for thy prayer is heard; and thy wife Elisabeth shall bear thee a son, and thou shalt call his name John.
> And thou shalt have joy and gladness; and many shall rejoice at his birth.
> For he shall be great in the sight of the Lord, and shall drink neither wine nor strong drink; and he shall be filled with the Holy Ghost, even from his mother's womb.
> And many of the children of Israel shall he turn to their Lord their God. *John* *Jesus*
> And he shall go before him in the spirit and power of Elias, to turn the hearts of the fathers to the children, and the disobedient to the wisdom of the just; to make ready a people prepared for the Lord. [Luke 1:13-17.]

In these words of the angel are several especially significant pronouncements:
1. the child should be named "John";
2. many should rejoice at his birth;
3. he should be great in the sight of the Lord;
4. he should be filled with the Holy Ghost even from his mother's womb;
5. he should turn many people to the Lord;
6. he should go forth in the spirit and power of Elias.

Each of these will be discussed in detail later; at this point it is sufficient to observe how wonderfully impressed and overwhelmed Zacharias must have been at such an announcement of the future activities of his unborn son.

In a latter-day revelation to the Prophet Joseph Smith the Lord reiterated three of the foregoing points:

> And also John the son of Zacharias, which Zacharias he (Elias) visited and gave promise that [1] he should have a son, and [2] his name should be John, and [3] he should be filled with the spirit of Elias. [D&C 27:7.]

John's Pre-Earth Appointment

The ancient prophets could not have spoken so definitely of John's forthcoming mission if it had not already been known and arranged in heaven. Concerning the matter of pre-earth appointment the Prophet Joseph Smith explained:

> Every man who has a calling to minister to the inhabitants of the

7

world was ordained to that very purpose in the Grand Council of heaven before this world was.[5]

One cannot avoid the conclusion that John's particular mission of being forerunner, baptizer, and witness for the Redeemer of the world was assigned to him in the Grand Council of heaven, and that such a mission could be entrusted only to a special person capable of carrying out the responsibility. John was without a doubt one of the noble and great ones who distinguished himself in the councils of heaven in the first estate, as shown to Abraham:

> Now the Lord had shown unto me, Abraham, the intelligences that were organized before the world was; and among all these there were many of the noble and great ones;
> And God saw these souls that they were good, and he stood in the midst of them, and he said: These I will make my rulers; for he stood among those that were spirits, and he saw that they were good; and he said unto me: Abraham, thou art one of them; thou wast chosen before thou wast born. [Abraham 3:22-23.]

Even as Abraham and Joseph Smith were chosen in the pre-earth life, we may be assured that so also was John, and certainly his earthly mission was appointed and explained to him in the Grand Council.

This preappointment, or foreordination, of one person often affects the appointment of many others, and establishes certain limits of time and distance. Since John was to be the forerunner of Jesus, it follows that he had to come to earth at a certain period of time and be in a particular geographical location. Furthermore, in keeping with the ancient law in Israel in the function of his priesthood, it was necessary that John be of the house of Aaron among the tribe of Levi. John's preappointment, therefore, had conditions and requirements that extended into mortality not only to his parents but much further back in the genealogical chain of his priestly lineage. More will be said of this in chapter three.

---

[5]*Teachings*, p. 365.

2
Palestine in the Meridian of Time

When the time arrived for the Messiah to come to earth in the flesh, it was also time for John, the forerunner, to begin his earthly mission and to take up the burden that had been placed upon his shoulders.

It was indeed a privilege to prepare the way before the very Son of God, to proclaim the gospel, to announce the presence of the Redeemer, and even to baptize him, but it was not an easy task. The covenant people of the Lord, the Jews among whom both Jesus and John would live, had fallen on hard times. The land of promise was not a free land; it was overrun and dominated by the Roman Empire, and upon the throne of Judah sat a "foreign" king — Herod, an Idumean, despised by Romans and Jews alike. No son of David ruled among the people of the Lord in the Lord's own land.

Even the covenant people themselves had wandered far from the precepts of the holy prophets. Jerusalem was bound by priestcraft, intrigue, self-righteousness, wickedness in high places, and rulers and priests who served themselves more than they served the people. It was not to be an easy thing for John, a mere man, to come among such men and conditions and prepare the way for the Son of God. Little wonder he is called a "voice . . . crying in the wilderness." It required a special kind of man to do what needed to be done — a man who was not only righteous and free from the taint and stain of sin, but courageous, bold, outspoken, forceful, plain, and forthright.

wilderness of Spirituality

Compare such as Saddam Hussein who invoked "Jihad" etc. as if he were an authorized cleric

It required power. These were sterner times than the average, and the mission required a man of sterner stuff than the average. He would have to be a man of power, comprehension, and determination. No doubt these traits were taken into consideration in the selection of this noble and great spirit when the assignment was made in the Grand Council.

The Law of Moses

There was seldom a complete separation between the religious and political history of Israel. The very nature of the kingdom and the source of its laws precluded that.

The children of Israel had a long national and family history. They looked with pride, and justly so, upon their descent from the patriarchs Abraham, Isaac, and Jacob. Their fathers had been slaves in Egypt and had been delivered out of bondage by Moses through the intervention and power of God. They had been shown God's mercy and love for the children of Israel. They had been given water from a rock and manna from heaven, and quails were sent when they wanted meat. They had been given a cloud and shadow by day and a pillar of fire by night.

From Mount Sinai God spoke to his people by fire, smoke, and his own voice, and gave many revelations "face to face" to his servant Moses (Exodus 33:11), who was both their political and ecclesiastical leader. But, in spite of all the tender mercies and spiritual manifestations, Israel as a people was obstinate, and was described by the Lord himself as having a neck of iron and a brow of brass (Isaiah 48:4). Israel often rejected the guidance that the God of Israel offered. If the counsel of God had been followed, it would have preserved the children of Israel as a people, free from the political bondage of other nations and free and independent in their social and religious dealings among themselves. But Israel preferred to go its own way.

When Moses descended from Mount Sinai he brought with him two stone tablets, on which were written, by the finger of God, not only the Ten Commandments, but also the laws and ordinances pertaining to the holy Melchizedek Priesthood. These were the saving ordinances of the gospel, and would have brought the people into the presence of God and the blessings of his kingdom. However, they proved by word and deed that they were unwilling and unable to receive the higher ordinances of the gospel; so the Lord provided for them a lesser law. Moses was called to the mount a second time, and there he received a very strict law "of performances and of ordinances" (Mosiah 13:30) which he was instructed to give unto the people in place of the higher ordinances they could have received had

10

they been worthy. This lesser law came to be known as the law of Moses.

This important historical event is explained in the Inspired Version of the Bible thus:

> And the Lord said unto Moses, Hew thee two other tables of stone, like unto the first, and I will write upon them also, the words of the law, according as they were written at the first on the tables which thou brakest; but it shall not be according to the first, for I will take away the priesthood out of their midst; therefore my holy order, and the ordinances thereof, shall not go before them; for my presence shall not go up in their midst, lest I destroy them.
>
> But I will give unto them the law as at the first, but it shall be after the law of a carnal commandment; for I have sworn in my wrath, that they shall not enter into my presence, into my rest, in the days of their pilgrimage. Therefore do as I have commanded thee, and be ready in the morning, and come up in the morning unto mount Sinai, and present thyself there to me, in the top of the mount. [Exodus 34:1-2, I.V.]

And again:

> At that time the Lord said unto me, Hew thee two other tables of stone like unto the first, and come up unto me upon the mount, and make thee an ark of wood.
>
> And I will write on the tables the words that were on the first tables, which thou breakest, save the words of the everlasting covenant of the holy priesthood, and thou shalt put them in the ark. [Deuteronomy 10:1-2, I.V.]

It appears that the Ten Commandments were written on both sets of tablets, and are part of the gospel as well as part of the law of Moses; however, the first tablets contained the ordinances of the Melchizedek Priesthood, while the second contained only those ordinances pertaining to what later became known as the Aaronic Priesthood.

This was the beginning of a special division of the priesthood called "Aaronic." Before that time there was only one priesthood comprehending the entire plan of salvation. The Prophet Joseph Smith clarified this relationship:

> Answer to the question, Was the Priesthood of Melchizedek taken away when Moses died? All Priesthood is Melchizedek, but there are different portions or degrees of it. That portion which brought Moses to speak with God face to face was taken away; but that which brought the ministry of angels remained. All the prophets had the Melchizedek Priesthood and were ordained by God himself.[6]

[6]*Teachings*, pp. 180-81.

11

Paul spoke of the law of Moses as a "schoolmaster," and explained that "it was added because of transgressions" (Galatians 3: 19-24). In other words, it was given to take the place of the higher law, to train and to discipline the children of Israel, in order to prepare them in the future for the greater portion of the gospel which their fathers could not or would not receive.

The Nephite prophet Abinadi ascribed a similar function to the law of Moses:

And now I say unto you that it was expedient that there should be a law given to the children of Israel, yea, even a very strict law; for they were a stiff-necked people, quick to do iniquity, and slow to remember the Lord their God;

Therefore there was a law given them, yea, a law of performances and of ordinances, a law which they were to observe strictly from day to day, to keep them in remembrance of God and their duty towards him.

But behold, I say unto you, that all these things were types of things to come.

And now, did they understand the law? I say unto you, Nay, they did not all understand the law; and this because of the hardness of their hearts; for they understood not that there could not any man be saved except it were through the redemption of God. [Mosiah 13:29-32.]

Although the Nephite prophets had the gospel of Jesus Christ, they understood that they must also continue in obedience to the performances of the law of Moses until Christ should come and fulfill the law. Abinadi explained:

And now ye have said that salvation cometh by the law of Moses. I say unto you that it is expedient that ye should keep the law of Moses as yet; but I say unto you, that the time shall come when it shall no more be expedient to keep the law of Moses. [Mosiah 13:27.]

Jacob also saw the law of Moses as preparatory, directing the people to the ultimate sacrifice of Jesus Christ:

Behold, they believed in Christ and worshiped the Father in his name, and also we worship the Father in his name. And for this intent we keep the law of Moses, it pointing our souls to him; and for this cause it is sanctified unto us for righteousness, even as it was accounted unto Abraham in the wilderness to be obedient unto the commands of God in offering up his son Isaac, which is a similitude of God and his Only Begotten Son. [Jacob 4:5.]

Nephi too declared this relationship between the law and the gospel:

And notwithstanding we believe in Christ, we keep the law of

12

Moses, and look forward with steadfastness unto Christ, until the law shall be fulfilled.

For, for this end was the law given; wherefore the law hath become dead unto us, and we are made alive in Christ because of our faith; yet we keep the law because of the commandments.

And we talk of Christ, we rejoice in Christ, we preach of Christ, we prophesy of Christ, and we write according to our prophecies, that our children may know to what source they may look for a remission of their sins.

Wherefore, we speak concerning the law that our children may know the deadness of the law; and they, by knowing the deadness of the law, may look forward unto that life which is in Christ, and know for what end the law was given. And after the law is fulfilled in Christ, that they need not harden their hearts against him when the law ought to be done away. [2 Nephi 25:24-27.]

Political History

After the time of Moses, a period of judges was established (Deborah, Samson, and so forth), but eventually the people of Israel desired to have a king, "like all the nations" (1 Samuel 8:4-5). Certain that such a course would lead to social and political trouble, Samuel the prophet-judge made solemn protest concerning it. The Lord, however, allowed them an earthly king because they desired it — but not until they had been sufficiently warned through Samuel of the Lord's displeasure (1 Samuel 8:6-22).

Three kings — Saul, David, and Solomon — successively ruled the twelve tribes, during which time Israel became a mighty nation and a prosperous people. After the death of Solomon (about 975 B.C.), however, the nation was divided by dissension and revolt over the burdensome taxation that had developed during Solomon's reign. The tribe of Judah, most of the tribe of Benjamin, and small remnants of a few other tribes followed the leadership of Rehoboam, the son of Solomon, and became known as the Kingdom of Judah, the Jews, or the Southern Kingdom. The other tribes followed Jeroboam, of the tribe of Ephraim, and became known as the Ten Tribes, the Kingdom of Israel, Ephraim, or the Northern Kingdom.

While the Kingdom of Judah remained in the area of Jerusalem and its surrounding territories, the Ten Tribes occupied primarily the land of Palestine northward, and for about 250 years both kingdoms functioned separately side by side. During this time there were kings of Israel and kings of Judah, and prophets of Israel and prophets of Judah. Elijah and Amos were prophets among the Northern Kingdom, or Kingdom of the Ten Tribes; Isaiah and Jeremiah were prophets among the Southern Kingdom, or Kingdom of Judah.

The very glorious kingdom of David was usurped, corrupt, from WITHIN

For the Jews to expect the Messiah to restore the former "Davidic glory" of Israel was ridiculous — when it had crumbled from WITHIN

13

During all this time, the Lord offered his covenant people divine instruction and manifestations of his concern for their welfare. The prophets among both houses of Israel warned of the political and social consequences of disobedience to divine laws and explained that the people would be brought into bondage to other nations unless they showed by their actions that they were truly the people of the Lord. But the children of Israel preferred to go their own way: they were well acquainted with pride and selfishness; the rich oppressed the poor, all the while professing a belief and respect for the God of heaven. They were proud of their national descent from righteous Abraham. They knew that God had led their fathers and saved them from many dangers. They wanted the Lord to do the same for them, but they did not want to pay the price of obedience to his commandments in order to obtain that kind of favor.

Then, in about 721 B.C., the prophets' predictions began to be fulfilled. The Kingdom of Israel was taken captive and scattered by the Assyrians and became lost as to any sort of national identity. Subsequently these people have come to be known as the "lost ten tribes." The Kingdom of Judah remained until about 589 B.C., but then it too was broken as a nation by Nebuchadnezzar, king of Babylon, and the Jews were carried away captive into Babylon.

The lost tribes have not to this day been restored as a people, but in the fifth century before Christ many of the Jews returned to Palestine under a decree from Cyrus the Persian, who had previously conquered Babylon.

Although those returning to Palestine sought to reestablish the kingdom of Judah in its former status and glory, they were never again a completely free and independent people. They were preyed upon by Greece, Egypt, and Syria, until finally under the leadership of Judas Maccabaeus, about 163-162 B.C., the people of Judah staged a revolt and gained a measure of political freedom. Their freedom lasted only about a century, however. In 63 B.C., during the reign of the Emperor Pompey, Judah came under the domination of the Romans. *only 66 (abt) yrs under Rome*

The Roman Empire allowed the Jews considerable social and religious freedom, but appointed Antipater, an Edomite and descendant of Esau — a race of people despised by the Jews — as the political leader. He was succeeded by his son, the brutal and cruel Herod the Great, who ruled Judah politically when John and Jesus were born.

Religious Developments

During Judah's political difficulties in the course of its reestablish-

14 *your parents or gr. parents wh have fought & in that war (ie WWII vets ....)*

ment in Palestine, things were happening to its religion also. Although the priestly organization and authority remained with the house of Aaron, there had been no prophet among them who could say "thus saith the Lord" since Malachi, who had lived about 400 B.C. The people had always been difficult, and hard to be taught spiritually, and this period of time was no exception. Without the immediate supervision of a prophet, Israel fell into ecclesiastical groups and parties. One of these, the *Pharisees*, is believed to have originated in the third century B.C., in the days preceding the Maccabean revolt against Greek domination. The Pharisees were the "puritans" of the time — the name means "separatist" — and were probably a reaction and protest to the tendencies of many of their countrymen to accept Greek culture and mannerisms. Their aim was to preserve strict conformity to the law of Moses. They became very exclusive and powerful in religious affairs, and had great influence among the masses of the people in Jesus' day. Among their beliefs was an acceptance of angels, spirits, immortality, and the resurrection from the dead.

PHARISEES: FORM IN PROTEST TO CONFORMITY TO GREEK CUSTOMS

Another party, arising about the same time as the Pharisees, but with different motives and ambitions, was the *Sadducees*. These were in favor of adopting Greek culture, and seem to have been guided largely by material and economic considerations. They were not as numerous as the Pharisees, but were more wealthy and more politically influential. They denied the existence of angels, spirits, immortality, and the resurrection.

Another prominent group among the Jews of that time were known as the *scribes*. These were basically copyists of the scriptures, but they made it their business to study and interpret as well as to copy. Because of their precise and detailed familiarity with the letter of the law, they were also called lawyers. The scribes were very numerous and influential and were not so much a separate group of their own but were drawn from among the Pharisees and Sadducees. Decisions and teachings of the scribes often became the oral law and tradition.

They knew HEBREW then most spoke ARAMAIC

Another order of the Jews, called the *Essenes*, is not mentioned in the New Testament but is known to us from other sources. Josephus describes the Essenes as extremely strict and exclusive.[7] Apparently they did not function actively among the cities of Palestine as did the Pharisees and Sadducees, but seem to have dwelt principally in settlements near the Dead Sea. The discovery of ancient scrolls (be-

---

[7]Flavius Josephus, *Antiquities of the Jews*, in *The Complete Works of Flavius Josephus*, trans. William Whiston (New York: Holt, Rinehart and Winston, n.d.), XVIII:1:5. *Antiquities of the Jews* is henceforth cited simply as *Antiquities*.

ANTIPATER
HEROD THE GREAT
HEROD

ginning in 1947) in that area has given considerable information about them.

Some political activists among the Jews in New Testament times were known as the *Herodians*. These seem to be more political than religious, but the very nature of Jewish theology precluded a clear separation between church and state in things Jewish at that time. The Herodians were probably Jews of influence who looked to Herod and his family as the most likely and practical means of maintaining Jewish independence from heavy foreign domination. Since they supported Herod's rule, they acquiesced somewhat to Roman control. They would probably have preferred to be completely independent, but Roman policy allowed the Jews some autonomy, and, perhaps for that reason, the Herodians were willing to support Roman rule through Herod. At least Roman control would offer them protection from the encroachment of other nations. But this approach would alienate them from the strong pro-Jewish nationalism of the Pharisees, Sadducees, and Essenes. Interestingly enough, though, the Pharisees were willing on occasion to unite with the Herodians against Jesus.

3

The Birth and Boyhood of John

In chapter one we discussed the pre-earth appointment of John in the Grand Council of heaven. In selection of the mortal lineage through which John would come to earth, there was some ancient law and procedure to be followed, for in order to be legally entitled to the priesthood of Aaron and to function as a priest under the law of Moses one had to be a literal descendant of Aaron. This was the rule as given to Moses:

> And thou shalt anoint Aaron and his sons, and consecrate them, that they may minister unto me in the priest's office. And thou shalt speak unto the children of Israel, saying, This shall be an holy anointing oil unto me throughout your generations. [Exodus 30:30-31.]

And concerning the sons of Aaron:

> And thou shalt anoint them, as thou didst anoint their father [Aaron], that they may minister unto me in the priest's office: for their anointing shall surely be an everlasting priesthood throughout their generations. [Exodus 40:15.]

Commenting on this procedure, the Prophet Joseph Smith explained:

> Here is a little of law which must be fulfilled. The Levitical Priesthood is forever hereditary — fixed on the head of Aaron and his sons forever, and was in active operation down to Zacharias the father of John.[8]

---

[8]*Teachings*, p. 319.

LINEAGE

ZACARIAS / ELIZABETH
AARON

MARY
DAVID

17

The things of the law of Moses, especially with regard to the qualifications of the priests and their functions in the offering of various animal sacrifices, were designed by revelation to prefigure and typify the Messiah and to bear witness of him. Heavy penalties were affixed to the performance of sacred rites and duties without the proper authority.[9] It was, therefore, essential that when the Messiah came in person as the Lamb of God, John, the forerunner and witness of the Lamb, should be of the proper lineage to qualify him for the mission. If it was necessary for a priest to be of the lineage of Aaron in order to labor with the sacrificial symbols, which were only prefigures of the Messiah, how much greater the necessity that John, the forerunner of the Messiah in person, be of the proper priestly lineage and authority.

The Lord, therefore, chose Zacharias, a priest of the family of Aaron, and Elisabeth, his wife, one of the "daughters of Aaron" (Luke 1:5), to be the mortal parents who would provide the right lineage to complete the inheritance — to bring about the proper combination of body and spirit. Zacharias belonged to the course of priests named after Abijah (later known as Abia).[10] This was the eighth of twenty-four courses established by David after the return from Babylon (1 Chronicles 24:10). Each course was appointed to serve a week in its turn at the temple. Because of the great number of priests, the honor came to relatively few, and seldom came twice to the same person. As the son of Zacharias and Elisabeth, John was fitted and qualified by earthly lineage and also by preappointment and foreordination. He was the right person to represent the law of Moses in its intended capacity as a schoolmaster to bring men unto Christ. He bridged two dispensations by being a legal representative of the law of Moses and at the same time being the one preappointed specifically to introduce and prepare the way for the coming of the Lord.

Miraculous Events Associated with John's Birth

Zacharias and Elisabeth were old and "well stricken in years" (Luke 1:7) and had no children. While Zacharias "executed the

---

[9]For example, see the judgment upon Korah and others, who took "too much upon" themselves in going beyond their assigned priesthood duties (Numbers 16:1-40), and the judgment against Uzza, who steadied the ark of God without having proper authority (1 Chronicles 13:7-10), and also upon king Uzziah, who burned incense in the temple, which pertained only to the priests, the sons of Aaron (2 Chronicles 26:16-21).

[10]This does not mean necessarily that Zacharias was a direct descendant of Abijah, but only that he belonged to the course that was named after him.

18

priest's office" in the temple, "in the order of his priesthood" (Luke 1:8, I.V.), the angel Gabriel appeared to him and said:

> Thy prayer is heard; and thy wife Elisabeth shall bear thee a son . . . .
> And thou shalt have joy and gladness; and many shall rejoice at his birth. [Luke 1:13-14.]

The basic fact of the angel's message is that they were soon to become parents of a choice son. There is, however, an implication that Zacharias and Elisabeth had yearned and prayed for children and now the Lord, having heard their prayer, was giving them a son befitting their faith and righteousness. The incident is reminiscent of Sarah, who bore Isaac in her old age, and Hannah, who, being childless, prayed for a son and was given Samuel. To be childless in Israel was looked upon as a great misfortune, and Elisabeth, when she knew she was with child, rejoiced saying:

> Thus hath the Lord dealt with me in the days wherein he looked on me, to take away my reproach among men. [Luke 1:25.]

Zacharias apparently doubted that he and Elisabeth could have a child in their old age, even though the angel had promised. Consequently, at the instigation of the angel, he was stricken dumb from that moment, as a sign that the words of the angel were true (Luke 1: 18-22).

A situation that occurred eight days after the child was born indicates that Zacharias, besides being unable to speak, may have become deaf. The angel had specified that the child should be named John, but some of the cousins and neighbors wanted to call him "Zacharias, after the name of his father" (Luke 1:59). To this Elisabeth objected. The people then

> made signs to his father, how he would have him called.
> And he asked for a writing table, and wrote, saying, His name is John. And they marvelled all.
> And his mouth was opened immediately, and his tongue loosed, and he spake, and praised God. [Luke 1:62-64.]

Particularly interesting is the fact that the people found it necessary to "make signs" to Zacharias to communicate with him. This is a strong suggestion that he was unable to *hear* them speak.

The birth of John was a well-publicized event. Zacharias was a prominent man in religious circles around Jerusalem, and was an officiating priest in the temple. The people knew of his vision of the angel and also of his subsequent inability to speak (Luke 1:21-22). Likewise, when Elisabeth gave birth to a son, "her neighbors and her cousins heard how the Lord had shewed great mercy upon her; and they rejoiced with her" (Luke 1:57-58). Furthermore, when the child was named and the affliction was removed from Zacharias many people knew about it. These events became frequent items of conversation throughout the area:

> And fear came on all that dwelt around about them: and all these sayings were noised abroad throughout all the hill country of Judea.
> And all they that heard them laid them up in their hearts, saying, What manner of child shall this be! And the hand of the Lord was with him. [Luke 1:65-66.]

Although public memory is usually very short, there must have been many in Israel who remembered these miraculous events connected with the birth of John. He would unavoidably be marked as a special child, and many would often be led to say, "What manner of child shall this be!"

The Eighth Day of John's Mortal Life

The eighth day of John's life was one of considerable importance. On this day he was circumcised (Luke 1:59) according to the law in Israel which the Lord had revealed to Abraham, specifying that it should be done when a child was eight days of age (Genesis 17:11-12). This was also the day on which he was officially given the name of "John" by Zacharias and Elisabeth over the protests of neighbors and relatives who thought he should be named Zacharias, after his father, as noted earlier.

Luke records that Zacharias, being filled with the Holy Ghost and the spirit of prophecy, gave a blessing to his son. Although the record does not specifically so state, it is implied that this blessing was given on the same eighth day of John's life. The words of Zacharias given on this occasion are known today as the "Benedictus" in Protestant and Catholic terminology. Zacharias's prophecy and blessing upon his son at this time included much concerning the mission to which John had been called and assigned in the pre-earth councils. The prophecy is in two parts. The first part (Luke 1:68-75) consists of praises to the Lord and speaks primarily of the future redemption and glory of Israel, as promised by God to Abraham and David and declared by the holy prophets:

> Blessed be the Lord God of Israel; for he hath visited and redeemed his people,
> And hath raised up an horn of salvation for us in the house of his servant David;
> As he spake by the mouth of his holy prophets, which have been since the world began:

That we should be saved from our enemies, and from the hand of all that hate us;

To perform the mercy promised to our fathers, and to remember his holy covenant;

The oath which he sware to our father Abraham,

That he would grant unto us, that we being delivered out of the hand of our enemies might serve him without fear,

In holiness and righteousness before him, all the days of our life.

The second part of the blessing (verses 76-79) is spoken directly to John:

And thou, child, shalt be called the prophet of the Highest: for thou shalt go before the face of the Lord to prepare his ways;

To give knowledge of salvation unto his people by the remission of their sins,

Through the tender mercy of our God; whereby the dayspring from on high hath visited us,

To give light to them that sit in darkness and in the shadow of death, to guide our feet into the way of peace.

The Inspired Version strengthens verse 77 in the following manner by placing an emphasis on baptism:

King James Version	Inspired Version
77 To give knowledge of salvation unto his people by the remission of their sins.	76 To give knowledge of salvation unto his people, *by baptism for* the remission of their sins.

Of notable interest in Zacharias's blessing upon John is the declaration that John would be called "the prophet of the Highest," that he would prepare the way before the Lord by giving "knowledge of salvation unto his people," and that he would give "light to them that sit in darkness." As John grew up to be a powerful preacher of the gospel, these predictions were amply fulfilled.

Still another event of the eighth day was a setting apart or ordination of John by an angel of God, whose identity is not revealed. This is recorded in the Doctrine and Covenants:

For he [John] was baptized while he was yet in his childhood, *and was ordained by the angel of God at the time he was eight days old unto this power, to overthrow the kingdom of the Jews,* and to make straight the way of the Lord before the face of his people, to prepare them for the coming of the Lord, in whose hand is given all power. [D&C 84:24.]

It is certainly unusual to ordain an infant eight days old to the priesthood, but whether this was actually a priesthood ordination or a setting apart to his special calling is not entirely clear. Although the word "ordain" is used, the nature of the event very much resembles what we today call a "setting apart." Zacharias was a priest after the order of Aaron and held true priesthood, and it would seem plausible that he would be the proper one to ordain his son. However, since John's particular calling was greater than that of any of his predecessors in the Aaronic order, it may be that no one then on earth (not even Zacharias) had the necessary keys to properly ordain and/or set him apart. Pres. Joseph Fielding Smith has explained the matter thus:

> The reason Zacharias could not ordain John is because of the fact that John received certain keys of authority which his father Zacharias did not possess. Therefore this special authority had to be conferred by this heavenly messenger, who was duly authorized and sent to confer it. John's ordination was not merely the bestowal of the Aaronic Priesthood, which his father held, but also the conferring of certain essential powers peculiar to the time among which was the authority to overthrow the kingdom of the Jews and "to make straight the way of the Lord." Moreover, it was to prepare the Jews and other Israelites for the coming of the Son of God. This great authority required a special ordination beyond the delegated power that had been given to Zacharias or any other priest who went before him, so the angel of the Lord was sent to John in his childhood to confer it.[11]

Bruce R. McConkie has written of the event in these words:

> In the case of John, he "was ordained by the angel of God at the time he was eight days old" — not to the Aaronic Priesthood, for such would come later, after his baptism and other preparation, but — "unto this power, to overthrow the kingdom of the Jews, and to make straight the way of the Lord before the face of his people, to prepare them for the coming of the Lord, in whose hand is given all power." (D&C 84:28.) That is, at this solemn eighth day ceremony, an angel, presumably Gabriel, gave the Lord's Elias the divine commission to serve as the greatest forerunner of all the ages.[12]

Even though an angel could ordain John to the priesthood, it is unlikely that an angel would have actually baptized him in water.[13]

---

[11]Smith, *Answers to Gospel Questions*, 5:2.

[12]Bruce R. McConkie, *Doctrinal New Testament Commentary*, 2 vols. (Salt Lake City: Bookcraft, 1965), 1:89.

[13]That angels do not perform water baptisms is discussed by the Prophet Joseph Smith as follows: "No wonder the angel told good old Cornelius that he must send for Peter to learn how to be saved: Peter could baptize, and angels could not, so long as there were legal officers in the flesh holding the keys of the kingdom" (*Teachings*, p. 265). The example of John the Baptist in conferring the priesthood upon Joseph Smith and Oliver Cowdery and then directing them to baptize each other under his supervision is likewise confirming evidence that angels do not perform baptisms in water for mortal beings. See Joseph Smith 2:70-71.

John's father would ordinarily be the right person to baptize him. However, John was surely not immersed when he was an infant only eight days old, and, as will be explained below, Zacharias was no longer living at the later time when it was proper for the baptism of John to take place. It is therefore probable that John was baptized by someone mortal holding the priesthood but who as yet is unidentified to us. That there were authorized persons on earth at the time is apparent. The Doctrine and Covenants (84:27) states that the Lord caused the Aaronic Priesthood to *continue* with the house of Aaron among the children of Israel *until* John" (italics added), which suggests that there would have been those of the house of Aaron among the Jews with enough authority to baptize. We know that Zacharias had the priesthood, but he would not have been the *only* one who had it. There were other priests holding the priesthood who also took their turn at the temple. The person or persons who ordained John to the Aaronic Priesthood and who also baptized him are not identified by name to us at the present, but this much is certain: John was both ordained and baptized, he grew physically and spiritually, and he "was in the deserts till the day of his shewing unto Israel" (Luke 1: 80). Thus the eighth day of John's mortal life was one of the busiest and most important of his ministry. The particular contribution of latter-day revelation is to certify to John's credentials, his authority, and his divine commission.

Herod's Edict of Death

Some time after the birth of Jesus, wise men from the east came to Jerusalem and inquired, "Where is he that is born King of the Jews? for we have seen his star in the east, and are come to worship him." When Herod the king (also called "the Great") heard of such a child he was troubled, and gathered "all the chief priests and scribes of the people together" and demanded of them where it was that the prophets had said Christ should be born (Matthew 2:1-4). The Inspired Version adds the comment at this point that Herod "greatly feared, yet he believed not the prophets" (Matthew 3:4).

Of course, the thing Herod so greatly feared was competition for his throne. He himself was king of the Jews, and the announcement that a new king of the Jews was born (and one not of his own household, at that) was a threat. Nor did the answer of the chief priests and scribes give him any relief, for they said the prophets had written that in Bethlehem there should "be born a prince" (Matthew 3:6, I.V.) who would rule and govern Israel (Matthew 2:3-6).

Feigning a desire to worship the new king, Herod asked the men from the east to find the child and then bring him word again. Guided by the star,[14] the wise men found the child and his mother and worshiped him themselves, but being instructed of God in a dream they returned to their own country by a different way and did not report to Herod.

Eventually realizing that the wise men were not going to bring him the information he desired, Herod was wroth and concocted a plan of action to destroy the young child. We can suppose that had the men from the east brought him word, Herod would have sent forth soldiers to slay Jesus in some way, either by stealth or by strong-arm tactics. However, being unable to identify the exact child, Herod was willing that all children in and around Bethlehem should be slain so that Jesus would be caught in the mass execution. Meanwhile time was passing, and so Herod "sent forth, and slew all the children that were in Bethlehem, and in all the coasts thereof, from two years old and under, according to the time which he had diligently enquired of the wise men" (Matthew 2:16).

How Jesus escaped this slaughter is familiar to us all: Joseph was warned in a dream to take Mary and Jesus into Egypt until Herod was dead. But how did John the son of Zacharias escape? John was approximately the same age as Jesus and lived in the approximate area of Bethlehem. The common knowledge that was had of the miraculous events attending his birth and the prospect of his future mission would surely have placed him under the suspicion of Herod and make him subject to the king's envy. The scriptures do not discuss John's relationship to Herod's edict, but the Prophet Joseph Smith did, and his words enlighten us considerably:

We will commence with John the Baptist. When Herod's edict went forth to destroy the young children, John was about six months older than Jesus, and came under the hellish edict, and Zacharias caused his mother to take him into the mountains, where he was raised on locusts and wild honey. When his father refused to disclose his hiding place, and being the officiating high priest at the Temple that year, [he] was slain by Herod's order, between the porch and the altar, as Jesus said.[15]

This very interesting explanation by the Prophet Joseph throws

---

[14]It seems reasonable that the star was not visible to others who might be in the vicinity, but to the wise men only. Subsequent events seem to dictate this, since it appears that only the wise men could find where the Christ child was, whereas if everyone could see and follow the star Herod would not have been so dependent on the men from the east to give him the location of the babe.

[15]*Teachings*, p. 261.

24

light on an otherwise mysterious passage in Matthew 23:35, wherein Jesus said:

> That upon you may come all the righteous blood shed upon the earth, from the blood of righteous Abel unto the blood of Zacharias son of Barachias, whom ye slew between the temple and the altar.

Bible commentators[16] have been at a loss to identify the "Zacharias" referred to in Matthew 23:35, but in the light of the Prophet's identification of the man as the father of John the Baptist, the passage takes on considerable historical meaning. Certainly the information given by the Prophet Joseph on this matter has a heart-touching effect on our appreciation of old Zacharias, who forfeited his own life to protect the life of his son, John. This heroic and faithful act dominates our mental image of Zacharias and supersedes the rather negative impression that is engendered by his earlier disbelief of the angel's words. When we remember Zacharias as a father and a protector even to the point of death, to us he will always be great.

There is an ancient tradition about the death of Zacharias that is similar to the foregoing explanation by the Prophet Joseph Smith. This is referred to by Anna Brownell Jameson in her book, *The History of Our Lord as Exemplified in Works of Art:*

> There is a very old tradition, as old at least as the 2nd century, that Herod also sought to destroy at the same time the son of Zacharias and Elizabeth — the young St. John, whose greatness had been foretold to him; that Elizabeth escaped with her son from amid the slaughter, and was afterwards miraculously preserved, and that Herod, in his rage at being thus baffled, sent and slew Zacharias between the altar and the Temple.[17]

The legend is also mentioned in New Testament apocryphal ma-

---

[16]See, for example, George Arthur Buttrick, et al., eds., *The Interpreter's Bible,* 12 vols. (New York: Abingdon Press, 1951), 7:540; D. Guthrie and J. A. Motyer, eds., *The New Bible Commentary Revised* (Grand Rapids: William B. Eerdmans Publishing Co., 1970), p. 845; J. R. Dummelow, ed., *A Commentary on the Holy Bible by Various Writers* (New York: The Macmillan Company, 1949), p. 701; and Raymond E. Brown, Joseph A. Fitzmyer, and Roland E. Murphy, eds., *The Jerome Biblical Commentary,* 2 vols. (Englewood Cliffs, N.J.: Prentice Hall, Inc., 1968), 2:103-4, all of which express difficulty in identifying the Zacharias mentioned in Matthew 23:35.

[17]London: Longman, Green, Longman, Roberts, & Green, 1865, p. 260. Mrs. Jameson continues: "In a Greek MS. in the Bibliothèque Impériale at Paris, with Byzantine miniatures of the 9th century, these events are simultaneously given. Here Herod and two counsellors are present, while one executioner and one child represent the massacre. In the same picture we see Zacharias being pierced with

terials.[18] On the strength of the credence given this topic by the Prophet Joseph Smith, we would be inclined to recognize an element of historical truth in this ancient tradition.

John's Boyhood

We know very little of John's youth and early manhood, but a few comments in the New Testament offer a clue to his austerity in food and clothing. The angel Gabriel told Zacharias that John would "drink neither wine nor strong drink" (Luke 1:15). Matthew says that John's clothing was of camel's hair with "a leathern girdle about his loins," and that his food "was locusts and wild honey" (Matthew 3:4). Jesus commented on the contrast between John's clothing and the soft raiment of those who "are gorgeously apparelled . . . in kings' courts" (Luke 7:25). Jesus also referred to John's diet, saying that "John the Baptist came neither eating bread not drinking wine" (Luke 7:33). Israel was oppressed by tyranny and

---

a lance, and Elizabeth and the young St. John enclosed in a rock, and seen only to the shoulders."

In describing works of art, Mrs. Jameson writes: "Elizabeth escapes with her son John from the Massacre at Bethlehem: in an attitude of fright, and clasping the child in her arms. . . . This incident, which is seldom omitted in Byzantine Art, is as seldom included in the more modern series. It occurs on the magnificent ivory triptych in the Louvre, and I have seen it in the background of a Flight into Egypt. It is also, I think, on the silver *dossale* which belongs to the Baptistery at Florence" (p. 292).

[18]Montague Rhodes James, trans., *The Apocryphal New Testament* (Oxford: The Clarendon Press, 1953), p. 48. In the Book of James, or Protevangelium, we find the following:

XXII. 1 But when Herod perceived that he was mocked by the wise men, he was wroth, and sent murderers, saying unto them: Slay the children from two years old and under. . . .

3 But Elizabeth when she heard that they sought for John, took him and went up into the hill-country and looked about her where she should hide him. . . .

XXIII. 1 Now Herod sought for John, and sent officers to Zacharias, saying: Where hast thou hidden thy son? And he answered and said unto them: I am a minister of God and attend continually upon the temple of the Lord: I know not where my son is. 2 And the officers departed and told Herod all these things. And Herod was wroth and said: His son is to be king over Israel. And he sent unto him again, saying: Say the truth: where is thy son? for thou knowest that thy blood is under my hand. And the officers departed and told him all these things. 3 And Zacharias said: I am a martyr of God if thou sheddest my blood: for my spirit the Lord shall receive, because thou sheddest innocent blood in the fore-court of the temple of the Lord.

And about the dawning of the day Zacharias was slain. And the children of Israel knew not that he was slain.

priestcraft, and perhaps John's observation of this situation caused in him a desire to be as unlike the proud Pharisees, the elaborate Sadducees, and those of kings' courts as possible. This might have influenced his choice of food and clothing. And, it might also be observed, what else could he wear and eat in the desert?

The Desert Years

As a result of the so-called Dead Sea Scrolls, some modern commentators who believe they have found a similarity in the theology of the Dead Sea "covenanters" and John the Baptist wish also to make a social connection. This is purely supposition, and there is no reliable basis for a conclusion that John was closely associated with any Dead Sea community. There is, however, an ancient tradition to the effect that John was left an orphan at an early age (due to the advanced age of his parents when he was born),[19] and was taken in or adopted by a desert community.[20] How accurate this tradition is we do not know, but there is a possibility of its occurrence. We have already mentioned the statement of the Prophet Joseph Smith concerning the death of Zacharias, which tends to confirm one old tradition, and it is possible that Elisabeth also might have died while John was still very young, in accordance with the other tradition.

It should be noted that the modern commentators who attempt to link John with the Dead Sea communities generally do so on the basis of a similarity of the teachings between John and the covenanters, with the suggestion that it was from the latter that John obtained his scriptural lessons and doctrine.[21] However, the tradition of John's

---

[19]This is is briefly referred to by Nahum Gale in his book *John the Baptist; or, The Prophet of the Highest* (Boston: American Tract Society, n.d.), p. 21. Says Gale: "It is perhaps owing to the tradition that John lost both his parents at an early age . . ."

[20]William H. Brownlee elaborates on this tradition in terms of the Dead Sea Scrolls of the Qumran community, and cites Josephus as saying that it was a common practice for the Essenes to adopt children ("John the Baptist in the New Light of Ancient Scrolls," Chapter 3 of *The Scrolls and the New Testament*, ed. Krister Stendahl [New York: Harper & Brothers, Publishers, 1957], p. 35).

[21]Some of the writers on this subject include William H. Brownlee, "A Comparison of the Covenanters of the Dead Sea Scrolls with Pre-Christian Jewish Sects," *The Biblical Archaeologist*, 13:50-72 (1950); Brownlee, "John the Baptist in the New Light of Ancient Scrolls," *Interpretation*, 9:71-90 (1955); and A. S. Geyser, "The Youth of John the Baptist," *New Testament*, 1:70-75 (1956). Geyser affirms that John's "outward appearance, words and acts betray the fact that he has been formed by one or other of the Essene sects inhabiting that very region between Khirbet-Qumran and Masada" (quoted in Charles H. H. Scobie, *John the Baptist* [Philadelphia: Fortress Press, 1964], pp. 58-59).

adoption concerns a *domestic* rather than a *theological* relationship, and asserts only that John's adoption by a desert community was for the purpose of preserving his life, and not for the purpose of religious indoctrination. That he was reared as a child by someone is certain, but, as will be seen shortly, he was taught the gospel by revelation from heaven. He no doubt was exposed to the desert people to some extent and knew of their beliefs and practices, but they would not have been the basic source of his spiritual knowledge.

John as a Levite and "Son of Aaron"

The records are silent as to John's training during his early years. As a Levite and descendant of Aaron, he most assuredly would be trained in the scriptures and in the work of a priest. Under the law of Moses a priest did not enter into the active ministry until about thirty years of age (Numbers 4:3; 1 Chronicles 23:3), but there would of necessity be much instruction and training beforehand. We can assume that whoever had charge of John as a youth would see that he attended to the usual lessons in scripture and history and the various school subjects current at the time in Israel. It is not necessary to think of John as a hermit and recluse separated from all society. The Dead Sea Scrolls have shown that there were several communities in the desert, and it was unlikely that John grew up entirely separated from all other human beings. His preaching to the Jews shows considerable acquaintance with tax collectors, soldiers, Sadducees, Pharisees, and the ways of men and things of the day.

It was customary in Israel for every boy to learn a trade, but since the Levites were set apart as a tribe to minister in the priesthood, this custom was not followed among them. It is probable, therefore, that John received no special training in this area.

John's preaching shows no direct or immediate association with the temple ritual and sacrifices. Certainly he understood the true meaning of these things and their proper place in the gospel plan, but his having grown up away from Jerusalem and the temple and his having been entrusted with a different *emphasis* in his ministry might possibly explain why the fragmentary account we have of his preaching does not make mention of it.

John at Age Twelve

We have no knowledge of John's activities as a youth. Even so, one wonders if he, even as Jesus, went up to Jerusalem at the Passover when he reached the age of twelve. At this age a boy became a "son of the Law,"[22] and it was a milestone in a boy's religious training to attend a passover service. Did John do so? If so, did he see his cousin Jesus there at the time? We do not know the answers to these questions, but it is interesting to reflect on the possibilities.

John and Jesus

We remember that Mary, the mother of Jesus, was "cousin" to Elisabeth, the mother of John, and she visited Elisabeth for three months just prior to John's birth. Both women were with child and both knew they would bear sons. Both children had been pre-announced and prenamed, and their individual missions had been defined by the angel Gabriel. These two women conversed with one another about the future missions and activities of their sons and knew of the relationship that would exist between them — one the Messiah, the other the forerunner to the Messiah (Luke 1:26-56; 2:21). Although the two children grew up in different parts of Palestine, surely each mother must have told her son something of the existence of the other boy. Whether John and Jesus ever met as boys we do not know, but there was considerable opportunity for them to know of one another through their mothers.[23]

At some future time we will certainly learn more of John's boyhood and early adult life, which will give us information about such things as marriage, family, educational training, travels, contact with groups, visions, revelations, and a great number of interesting items.

The Mind of John

We wonder also what thoughts may have raced through the mind of John while he studied the scriptures during the years of his preparation in the desert. In his travels he must often have seen Mount Nebo, from whose peak Moses had viewed the Land of Promise and spoken of the promised Messiah. He was at times perhaps not far from the

---

[22]The Talmud specifies that after the twelfth year a boy becomes a youth and is to observe the fast on the Day of Atonement. There is also a legend that Moses left his home when he was twelve, and Josephus says that Samuel began to prophesy when he was twelve (*Antiquities*, V:10:4). This is closely allied to the Jewish term *Bar Mitzvah*, which denotes a young man reaching the age of religious maturity or accountability. From that time on he is considered an adult in religious aspects, and becomes a "son of the Law," or "son of the commandments." See Philip Birnbaum, *A Book of Jewish Concepts* (New York: Hebrew Publishing Co., 1964), pp. 94-95.

[23]"A painting in the Berlin Gallery illustrates the legend, related by St. Bonaventura, that when the Virgin and Joseph returned from Egypt, with the Child Jesus, they met the young Baptist upon the skirts of the wilderness" (Gale, *John the Baptist*, p. 22).

place where Joshua crossed the Jordan. He lived in the general area where Amos had pastured his flocks, and where Elijah was fed by the ravens. In such a historic geographical area of Israel's prophets, he must have many times reflected on his own destiny, yet to be unfolded — to announce the coming of the Son of God, who was worshiped by the prophets and who was greater than any of them.

The record states that John was "filled with the Holy Ghost from his mother's womb" (D&C 84:27; also Luke 1:15). This fact no doubt was a great factor in his training and preparation. "The Holy Ghost is a revelator," and "no man can receive the Holy Ghost without receiving revelations."[24] Through the years the Holy Ghost was preparing John's mind to understand his mission and to carry it forth. His clear and accurate knowledge of the gospel — which will be discussed in the next two chapters — attests to the quality of the instruction which he received during these important years in the desert. John possessed the keys of the Aaronic Priesthood, which "holds the keys of the ministering of angels" (D&C 13), and it follows that, in addition to his ordination by an angel when he was eight days old, he would receive the visitation of angels during these preparatory years. Elder James E. Talmage agrees:

> He had been a student under the tutelage of divine teachers; and there in the wilderness of Judea the word of the Lord reached him; as in similar environment it had reached Moses and Elijah of old.[25]

The training of the herald and forerunner of the Messiah required the finest and most effective spiritual education possible and included such things as study of the scriptures, lessons in Israel's history, the workings and revelations of the Holy Ghost, and the ministry of angels. When John came forth preaching at the age of thirty, he was ready. He knew what his mission was and what he must do, and he had the authority to go about it — which is the case with all of the Lord's true prophets who are engaged in setting up the kingdom of God upon the earth.

---

[24]*Teachings*, p. 328.
[25]*Jesus the Christ* (Salt Lake City: Deseret Book Company, 1956), p. 122.

4

John's Public Ministry[26]

The Beginning of John's Public Ministry

As stated in chapter three, there are many things we do not know about John's youth and early manhood. Latter-day revelation adds some information about him, but it is mostly doctrinal rather than historical. However, one very significant contribution of latter-day revelation is that it certifies John's credentials as a prophet and his divine authority to carry out his appointed mission. When the proper time arrived for John to come among the people he was fully qualified, prepared, and mature.

Matthew's account in the King James Version seems to start John on his public ministry a little too early. After relating the story of Joseph, Mary, and Jesus coming out of Egypt and going to Nazareth to live (Matthew 2:19-23), Matthew adds: "In those days came John the Baptist, preaching in the wilderness of Judaea" (Matthew 3:1). Although we do not know Jesus' exact age when the family left Egypt, we do know that King Herod lived only a short time, perhaps a year or two, after issuing the edict to slay the Bethlehem children — which was the whole cause of the trip to Egypt anyway — and there would be no need for Jesus to stay in Egypt after Herod was dead. It would

---

[26]The emphasis in this chapter is primarily historical and non-doctrinal. The doctrinal and theological implications of John's preaching are considered in detail in chapter five.

be a conservative estimate, therefore, that Jesus was no more than five years of age when the family settled in Nazareth, and he was probably younger. The scripture says he was a "young child" (Matthew 2:21). John was a mere six months older than Jesus, which at best would make him five and a half or six years old, and it is highly improbable that he was preaching the gospel at such an early age. More than twenty-five years, then, would actually still elapse before John came preaching. Twenty-five years are simply too many to be casually dismissed as being "in those days."

This situation is remedied in the Inspired Version of Matthew by the insertion of a statement that Jesus grew to maturity while at Nazareth and that "after many years, the hour of his ministry drew nigh." This important information is followed by the declaration that it was "in those days" (after Jesus had grown to maturity) that John the Baptist came preaching.

The following comparison demonstrates how the Inspired Version is helpful in covering the transitional years from childhood to manhood for Jesus and therefore the same period for John.

Kings James Version	Inspired Version
Matt. 2:19 But when Herod was dead, behold, an angel of the Lord appeareth in a dream to Joseph in Egypt,	Matt. 3:19 But when Herod was dead, behold, an angel of the Lord appeared in a vision to Joseph in Egypt,
20 Saying, Arise, and take the young child and his mother, and go into the land of Israel: for they are dead which sought the young child's life.	20 Saying, Arise, and take the young child and his mother, and go into the land of Israel; for they are dead who sought the young child's life.
21 And he arose, and took the young child and his mother, and came into the land of Israel. . . .	21 And he arose, and took the young child and his mother, and came into the land of Israel. . . .
23 And he came and dwelt in a city called Nazareth: that it might be fullfilled which was spoken by the prophets, He shall be called a Nazarene.	23 And he came and dwelt in a city called Nazareth, that it might be fulfilled which was spoken by the prophets, He shall be called a Nazarene.
	24 And it came to pass that Jesus grew up with his brethren, and waxed strong, and waited upon the Lord for the time of his ministry to come.
	25 And he served under his father, and he spake not as other men, neither could he be taught;

for he needed not that any man should teach him.

26 And after many years, the hour of his ministry drew nigh.

Matt. 3:1 In those days came John the Baptist, preaching in the wilderness of Judaea.

27 And in those days came John the Baptist, preaching in the wilderness of Judea.

This correction is necessary for more than one reason. Not only is it desirable that young John be given time to grow to manhood before beginning his public ministry, but the present King James translation of Matthew's account does not (1) permit John to comply with the provisions of the law of Moses or (2) agree with a careful time-table given by Luke.

In the law given to Moses, it was specified that a Levite should begin his priestal ministry at about age thirty (Numbers 4:3; 1 Chronicles 23:3). Since John was a Levite, this would apply to him, and accordingly when he was about thirty years of age "the word of God came unto John the son of Zacharias in the wilderness" (Luke 3:2).

Luke lists six separate items by which he establishes the setting for the beginning of John's ministry:

[1] Now in the fifteenth year of the reign of Tiberius Caesar, [2] Pontius Pilate being governor of Judaea, and [3] Herod being tetrarch of Galilee, and [4] his brother Philip tetrarch of Ituraea and of the region of Trachonitis, and [5] Lysanias the tetrarch of Abilene, [6] Annas and Caiaphas being the high priests, the word of God came unto John the son of Zacharias in the wilderness. [Luke 3:1-2.]

The Inspired Version adds the following clarification to verse two:

King James Version	Inspired Version
2 . . . the word of God came unto John the son of Zacharias in the wilderness.	2 *Now in this same year,* the word of God came unto John, the son of Zacharias, in the wilderness. [Italics added.]

The "fifteenth year of the reign of Tiberius Caesar" is thought by scholars to be approximately A.D. 26; thus John's ministry dates from about that time.[27]

_____

[27]Luke's accuracy as a historian is praised by biblical scholars and archaeologists. Even supposed difficulties concerning "Lysanias the tetrarch of Abilene" (Luke 3:1) have largely been resolved. See F. F. Bruce, *The New Testament Documents: Are They Reliable?* (Grand Rapids: William B. Eerdmans Publishing Co., 1965), pp. 87-88; J. A. Thompson, *The Bible and Archaeology* (Grand Rapids: William B. Eerdmans Publishing Co., 1962), pp. 377-78; James Montgomery Boice, "The

The detailed manner in which Luke identifies the beginning of John's ministry suggests the importance that he placed on John's work. Furthermore, Mark opens his account with the words, "The beginning of the Gospel of Jesus Christ, the Son of God" (Mark 1:1), and proceeds immediately to tell of the preaching of John the Baptist. The fourth Gospel introduces John as an adult and devotes most of the first chapter to his ministry. The matter is emphasized again in Acts 1:22, wherein Peter specifies the starting date for the believers as "beginning from the baptism of John."

Large crowds came to hear John, "preaching in the wilderness of Judaea" near the shores of the Jordan River. While Matthew, Mark, and Luke say simply that John baptized in the wilderness in the region round about Jordan, the fourth Gospel specifies that John baptized at "Bethabara beyond Jordan" (John 1:28). This location is also mentioned in the account of the vision given to Lehi 600 years before John's time, referred to in 1 Nephi 10:9.[28] "Then went out to him," says Matthew, "Jerusalem, and all Judea, and all the region round about Jordan, and many were baptized of him in Jordan confessing their sins" (Matthew 3:31-32, I.V.).

Many Pharisees and Sadducees, however, came to his baptism without repentance, claiming spiritual supremacy on the basis alone of being descendants of Abraham (Matthew 3:7-9; Luke 3:7-8). These John rebuked. "The ax," he declared, "is laid unto the root of the trees: therefore every tree which bringeth not forth good fruit is hewn down, and cast into the fire" (Matthew 3:10; also Luke 3:9).

In addition to the Pharisees and Sadducees, among the multitudes who came to John were publicans (Luke 3:12), soldiers (Luke 3:14), and harlots (Matthew 21:32). John was very popular with the people. "All" men held him as a prophet (Matthew 21:26; John 4:2, I.V.), and even "were in expectation, and . . . mused in their hearts of John, whether he were the Christ, or not" (Luke 3:15). But John was careful to explain to them all:

> I indeed baptize you with water; but one mightier than I cometh, the latchet of whose shoes I am not worthy to unloose: he shall baptize you with the Holy Ghost and with fire. [Luke 3:16.]

Reliability of the Writings of Luke and Paul," *Christianity Today*, 24 November 1967, pp. 8-10.

[28]In many translations of the Bible since the King James Version, John 1:28 reads "Bethany" rather than "Bethabara." However, this could not have reference to the well-known Bethany which is two miles east of Jerusalem, and must refer to another Bethany east of (or beyond) the Jordan. The Lamsa translation from Aramaic reads: "These things happened in Bethany at the Jordan crossing, where John was baptizing."

Baptism of Jesus

Then Jesus came from Nazareth to the Jordan and requested baptism of John. How long John had been preaching and baptizing before this visit is not specified. Although it need not have been an excessive time, probably several months would be required for John to have stirred up so many people and to have accomplished a work of the proportions indicated in the records.

Out of humility and meekness, John at first hesitated, saying that he had need to be baptized of Jesus. He finally acceded to the Savior's request, however, and when Jesus came out of the water and prayed, John saw the Holy Ghost in the sign of a dove descend from heaven upon Jesus. As John himself later explained, he had had direct revelation about baptizing Jesus, and this had been a preappointed sign designated to him as the positive evidence by which he would know that he had baptized the Son of God (John 1:32-34).

At the same time a voice spoke from heaven saying, "This is my Beloved Son"[29] (Matthew 3:17). Until this time John had declared that the Messiah *would come,* but from this moment forward he would declare that the Messiah *had already come* among them.

Soon after being baptized by John, Jesus went into the wilderness for forty days and "communed with God" (Matthew 4:1-2, I.V.).[30]

John as a Forerunner and a Witness

The accounts given in Matthew, Mark, and Luke tell of John's preaching to "prepare . . . the way" for the Lord, whereas the fourth Gospel emphasizes that John came to "bear witness" of the Lord. These are two different points of emphasis, and are complementary rather than exclusive of one another. The difference between them is that Matthew, Mark, and Luke deal with John's ministry *before* he baptized Jesus, and therefore emphasize preparing the way, while the fourth Gospel deals with John's ministry *after* he baptized Jesus, and hence the emphasis on being a witness. Jesus' forty-day experience

---

[29]It is probable that the sign of the dove and also the voice of the Father were witnessed by John and Jesus alone and not observed by any who might be standing by. These are not events that the casual onlooker is privileged to enjoy. The "dove" was a sign to John, the voice a matter of approval to Jesus and to John.

[30]The Inspired Version gives a different concept of Jesus' forty-day sojourn in the wilderness than is obtained from the King James Version. In the latter Jesus is reported to have gone into the wilderness "to be tempted of the devil" (Matthew 4:1), and to have been "forty days tempted of the devil" (Luke 4:2). The Inspired Version reads that Jesus went into the wilderness "to be with God," and that after he had fasted forty days and "had communed with God" he was then tempted of the devil (Matthew 4:1-2; Luke 4:2).

in the wilderness can probably be placed between these two basic parts of John's testimony concerning him.

The following passages illustrate the "before" and "after" segments of John's teaching. Although the separation is discernible from the King James Version, the Inspired Version makes the point clearer and is, therefore, included, where applicable, for comparison.

Kings James Version	Inspired Version
Matt. 3:11 I indeed baptize you with water unto repentance: but he that cometh after me is mightier than I, whose shoes I am not worthy to bear: he shall baptize you with the Holy Ghost, and with fire:	Matt. 3:38 I indeed baptize you with water, *upon your repentance; and when he of whom I bear record* cometh, *who* is mightier than I, whose shoes I am not worthy to bear, (*or whose place I am not able to fill,) as I said, I indeed baptize you before he cometh, that when he cometh he may* baptize you with the Holy Ghost and fire.
12 Whose fan is in his hand, . . .	39 *And it is he of whom I shall bear record,* whose fan *shall be* in his hand, . . .
	40 Thus came John, preaching and baptizing in the river of Jordan; bearing record, that he who was coming after him had power to baptize with the Holy Ghost and fire.
13 Then cometh Jesus from Galilee to Jordan unto John, to be baptized of him.	41 *And* then cometh Jesus from Galilee to Jordan, unto John, to be baptized of him.

It is evident in the foregoing account that John the Baptist's words were spoken before, and in anticipation of, the coming of Jesus. Mark and Luke give the same setting as Matthew, but the Gospel of John presents quite a different setting:

King James Version	Inspired Version
John 1:6 There was a man sent from God, whose name was John.	John 1:6 There was a man sent from God, whose name was John.
7 The same came for a witness, to bear witness of the Light, that all men through him might believe.	7 The same came *into the world* for a witness, to bear witness of the light, *to bear record of the gospel through the Son, unto all,* that through him men might believe.

8 He was not that Light, but was sent to bear witness of that Light. . . .

15 John bare witness of him, and cried, saying, This was he of whom I spake, He that cometh after me is preferred before me: for he was before me. . . .

32 And John bare record, saying, I saw the Spirit descending from heaven like a dove, and it abode upon him.

33 And I knew him not: but he that sent me to baptize with water, the same said unto me, Upon whom thou shalt see the Spirit descending, and remaining on him, the same is he which baptizeth with the Holy Ghost.

34 And I saw, and bare record that this is the Son of God.

8 He was not that light, but *came* to bear witness of that light. . . .

15 John bear [sic] witness of him, and cried, saying, This *is* he of whom I spake; He *who* cometh after me, is preferred before me; for he was before me. . . .

31 And John bare record, saying; *When he was baptized of me,* I saw the Spirit descending from heaven like a dove, and it abode upon him.

32 And I knew him; *for* he *who* sent me to baptize with water, the same said unto me; Upon whom thou shalt see the Spirit descending, and remaining on him, the same is he *who* baptizeth with the Holy Ghost.

33 And I saw, and bare record that this is the Son of God.

Here it is plain that John spoke of an event that had already taken place: he had baptized the Messiah and was a qualified witness. It is interesting that the records of Matthew, Mark, and Luke tell only of that part of John's ministry which came *before* he baptized Jesus, while the Gospel of John describes only the part which came *afterwards*.

Actually, John's public ministry had three phases: (1) proclaiming that Jesus *would* come, (2) announcing that Jesus *had* come, and finally (3) teaching his own disciples and converts. We have already considered the first two items, and will now turn our attention to the third.

John and His Disciples

During his public ministry John gathered followers, or disciples, who called him "Rabbi" (John 3:26), and whom he taught to fast (Matthew 9:14; Mark 2:18, Luke 5:33) and to pray (Luke 11:1). At John's own urging, many of his disciples left him and followed Jesus, but some stayed with him even though he made it plain that he was not the Messiah. There were still disciples attached to John at the time of his death, which was at least a year and a half after he baptized Jesus (Matthew 14:12, Mark 6:29).

Some of those who first followed John are later found among the twelve whom Jesus selected as apostles. One of these is John, the brother of James, and another is Andrew, the brother of Peter. These two men were first disciples of John the Baptist, and it was through him that they became acquainted with Jesus. The account of their departure from John and attachment to Jesus is as follows:

Again the next day after John stood, and two of his disciples;
And looking upon Jesus as he walked, he saith, Behold the Lamb of God!
And the two disciples heard him speak, and they followed Jesus.
Then Jesus turned, and saw them following, and saith unto them, What seek ye? They said unto him, Rabbi, (which is to say, being interpreted, Master,) where dwellest thou?
He saith unto them, Come and see. They came and saw where he dwelt, and abode with him that day: for it was about the tenth hour.
One of the two which heard John speak, and followed him, was Andrew, Simon Peter's brother.
He first findeth his own brother Simon, and saith unto him, We have found the Messias, which is, being interpreted, the Christ. [John 1:35-41.]

It will be noted that Andrew is mentioned by name. Although the record does not specifically give the name of the other disciple, it is characteristic of John the Beloved frequently to make indirect mention of himself while remaining technically anonymous. (For example compare John 13:23; 18:15; 19:26-27; 20:2-8; 21:7, 20, 24.)

How many others among the Twelve were first disciples of John the Baptist we do not know, but a statement attributed to Peter might imply that many, if not all, of the Twelve had once been John's followers. After telling the disciples — about 120 in number — of Judas's apostasy and death, Peter indicated that another must be chosen and appointed in Judas's place and be numbered among the Twelve. Peter continued:

Wherefore of these men which have companied with us all the time that the Lord Jesus went in and out among us,
Beginning from the baptism of John, unto that same day that he was taken up from us, must one be ordained to be a witness with us of his resurrection. [Acts 1:21-22.]

This suggests that there were a number of men among the disciples of Jesus then present who had been together as disciples from the baptism of John on through the years and events up until and including Jesus' ascension.

That John continued to preach and also to baptize even after he baptized Jesus is evident from several passages and is especially clear in John 3:22-24:

> After these things came Jesus and his disciples into the land of Judaea; and there he tarried with them, and baptized.
> And John also was baptizing in Aenon near to Salim, because there was much water there: and they came, and were baptized.
> For John was not yet cast into prison.

The geographical location of "Aenon near to Salim" is not certain. There were several places named Salim.[31] Some commentators place it north of Judea in Samaria. Others think it was north of Jericho near the Jordan River in Perea, or even in Decapolis. John's popularity and his influence with great numbers of disciples may possibly have begun to annoy Herod Antipas, causing Herod to fear John's mounting political power. If so, John may have fled to Aenon to escape Herod's wrath, and in that case Samaria would be the better of the two mentioned locations, since the Salim in Perea was still in Herod's jurisdiction. If John, then, was in Samaria baptizing with his disciples, he might have laid the groundwork for Jesus' later successful ministry in Samaria, as described in John 4:3-43.

Did John's Disciples Perform Baptisms?

For a time John and his disciples worked alongside Jesus and his disciples; that is, their ministries overlapped for a short period after Jesus' baptism and until John's imprisonment. This is clearly portrayed in the previously quoted passage about John at "Aenon near to Salim." It was a time of great activity, with many conversions and baptisms, and it is written that "Jesus made and baptized more disciples than John" (John 4:1). The Inspired Version explains that Jesus did not do all of this baptizing himself but rather that he delegated the privilege as "an example" to his disciples. As a consequence, his disciples baptized more people than he himself did (John 4:3, I.V.).

This period of baptizing by the disciples of Jesus was shortly before the call of the Twelve. No doubt Jesus had ordained some of his disciples to a priesthood office with sufficient authority to baptize, prior to and preparatory to their subsequent call to the apostleship. It is unlikely that men would be called directly into the Twelve without previous instruction, and these passages show that Jesus' disciples did receive instruction and experience before their higher appointment and ordination.

---

[31]The location of "Aenon near to Salim" is discussed in detail in chapter seven.

39

The question then arises whether the disciples of John also performed baptisms. There is no direct affirmation that they did. It may be that John did all of the baptizing himself, and yet it seems possible that he might have ordained some of his disciples to assist. This we do not know. An objection to the theory that the disciples of John performed baptisms might be raised on the grounds that this would produce a "rival" or "competing" group to Jesus. But why, then, did Jesus permit John to continue to baptize? And if John could continue, could not also his disciples if properly ordained? Since John was anxious for them to leave him and follow Jesus, however, it seems unlikely that John's disciples would be given authority to baptize. When they became Jesus' disciples, they could then "come in at the gate and be ordained" to preach the gospel and perform the ordinances thereof. (Compare D&C 42:11; 43:7.)

John's Last Recorded Testimony

John's last recorded testimony of Jesus was given to his own disciples shortly before his imprisonment (John 3:25-36). Apparently while John was at "Aenon near to Salim" there "arose a question between some of John's disciples and the Jews about purifying [baptism?]." They came to John and said:

> Rabbi, he that was with thee beyond Jordan, to whom thou barest witness, behold, the same baptizeth, and all men come to him. [John 3:26.]

The greatness of John's soul and his unselfish loyalty to the Master are displayed in his reply:

> A man can receive nothing, except it be given him from heaven.
> Ye yourselves bear me witness, that I said, I am not the Christ, but that I am sent before him.
> He that hath the bride is the bridegroom: but the friend of the bridegroom, which standeth and heareth him, rejoiceth greatly because of the bridegroom's voice: this my joy therefore is fulfilled.
> He must increase, but I must decrease.
> He that cometh from above is above all: he that is of the earth is earthly, and speaketh of the earth: he that cometh from heaven is above all.
> And what he hath seen and heard, that he testifieth; and no man receiveth his testimony.
> He that hath received his testimony hath set to his seal that God is true.
> For he whom God hath sent speaketh the words of God: for God giveth not the Spirit by measure unto him.
> The Father loveth the Son, and hath given all things into his hand.

He that believeth on the Son hath everlasting life: and he that believeth not the Son shall not see life; but the wrath of God abideth on him. [John 3:27-36.]

John's loyalty and humility are nowhere better described than in this instance. It is natural for a man to want to project himself, but John was frank and quick to remind his disciples again that he was not the Christ but had borne witness of the Christ. He was not the Bridegroom, but only the "friend of the Bridegroom." His joy was in knowing that he had made things ready for the Bridegroom. The great expression of John's heart is found in the words "He must increase, but I must decrease" (verse 30).

Most commentators question whether verses 31-36 are the words of the Baptist or a commentary by John the Beloved. However, we could probably conclude that they are the words of John the Baptist. A detailed analysis of this matter is given in chapter five in a discussion of John the Baptist's knowledge of the gospel, and in chapter six concerning the "Record of John."

The Length of John's Public Ministry

The length of John's public ministry is not clearly delineated in the scriptures, but it would certainly have required several months before and several months after the baptism of Jesus. There are two principal dates with which we have to work. The first is the announcement in Luke 3:2 (I.V.) that in the "same year," which was "the fifteenth year of the reign of Tiberias," the word of God came to John and he began to preach. This appears to be A.D. 26.[32]

The other date of significance for determining the length of John's public ministry is the date of his imprisonment, which also precipitated the close of Jesus' early Judean ministry and is calculated by scholars as December, A.D. 27. If these dates are correct, John's ministry spanned not less than twelve and not more than twenty-four months.

A third date has to do with Jesus' baptism, and is based on the assumption that Jesus was baptized near his thirtieth birthday. Since it is common in Christendom to accept December as the month of Jesus' birth, some commentators place the baptism of Jesus in December, A.D. 26. Accepting April as the month of Jesus' birth, however, we could probably place the baptism of Jesus in April, A.D. 27. Since there is only one year from 1 B.C. to A.D. 1, and we are using 4 B.C. as the birth of Christ, the year A.D. 27 would possibly be Jesus' thirtieth year.

---

[32]Precise dating is difficult. A discussion of Luke's accuracy in dating the beginning of John's ministry is found in note 27.

Since John had begun his public ministry several months before baptizing Jesus, it is assumed that John began his public ministry in the summer of A.D. 26, and it came to a close about eighteen months later, in the late fall or early winter of A.D. 27, at the time he was imprisoned. This allows John approximately nine months of public ministry before the baptism of Jesus and approximately an additional nine months of public ministry until he was imprisoned.

John and Herod Antipas

Herod Antipas was the son of Herod the Great. While it appears that Antipas and Jesus met but once, at which time Jesus refused to speak with him (Luke 23:6-11), Antipas and John seem to have had many contacts with one another. The record states that Herod Antipas listened to John, and also feared and respected him and "did many things for him." The Inspired Version gives the best account of the relationship between John and Herod Antipas and is presented below with the King James Version included for comparison:

King James Version	Inspired Version
Mark 6:20 For Herod feared John, knowing that he was a just man and an holy, and observed him; and when he heard him, he did many things, and heard him gladly.	Mark 6:21 For Herod feared John, knowing that he was a just man, and a holy *man, and one who feared God* and observed *to worship* him; and when he heard him he did many things *for him*, and heard him gladly.

What the "many things" are that Herod did for John we do not know, but a marginal reading in the King James Version gives an alternate reading for the phrase "and observed him" and suggests that the meaning could also be that Herod "kept him" or "saved him." Lamsa's translation from Aramaic manuscripts renders this passage, "For Herod was afraid of John, because he knew that he was a righteous and holy man, and he guarded him." The Catholic (Confraternity) version reads that Herod "protected" him. So also does Luther's German translation. The general impression conveyed by the foregoing passage from Mark is that Herod had a certain awesome respect for John as a prophet, and even had moments when he liked to listen to him. When Herodias was angry with John and would have killed him, Herod, awed by John's righteousness, protected him from Herodias for a time. It is certain, however, that this was a "sometime" attitude and that Herod did not wish to follow John wholeheartedly.

42

John and the Pharisees

John had frequent contact with the Pharisees, generally in un-friendly circumstances. The earliest instance of which we have a record is the coming of the Pharisees and Sadducees to John's baptism without the fruits of repentance, at which time John accused them of being a "generation of vipers" (Matthew 3:7).

At another time the Sanhedrin sent a delegation of Pharisees to John in Bethabara to ask him who he thought he was and why he was baptizing the people (John 1:19-25). It does not appear that they were willing to accept John's testimony, but neither does the tone of this encounter seem particularly unfriendly or harsh. Jesus himself later referred to this event and reminded the Pharisees that they had "sent unto John" and that for a while they had been willing to listen to John (John 5:33-35).

Later, while John was in prison, Jesus spoke to the multitudes and extolled John's great mission. The scripture says that "the people that heard him, and the publicans, justified God," because they had been "baptized with the baptism of John," but the "Pharisees and lawyers rejected the counsel of God . . . , being not baptized of [John]" (Luke 7:29-30).

The words of Jesus also imply that the Pharisees had said that John "hath a devil" (Luke 7:33).

Still later, after John was dead, Jesus spoke to the Pharisees about John's authority to baptize, which they stubbornly refused to ac-knowledge. Publicans and harlots, he said, would go into heaven be-fore the Pharisees, because the publicans and harlots had believed John and the Pharisees had not. The Savior then added the sharpened comment that the Pharisees ought to have observed a lesson in re-pentance from the good example of the publicans and harlots (Mat-thew 21:23-32).

We know that the Pharisees were a major factor in the arrest and crucifixion of Jesus; as will be observed in chapter seven, they were probably instrumental in the arrest of John also.

John's Widespread Influence

John made a strong impression in his relatively short ministry, and his influence was felt at great distances. The bulk of his ministry seems to have been spent near the Jordan River, but, as noted earlier, there is strong probability that he traveled into Samaria also. While Jesus was in Galilee, the disciples of John from that area approached him about fasting (Matthew 9:14). Furthermore, Andrew and John the Beloved, as we have already noted, were once disciples of John the Baptist, and they were both from Galilee.

Twenty years later, when Paul was at Ephesus (about A.D. 54-55) he found "certain disciples" who claimed to have had "John's baptism" (Acts 19:1-7). As it turned out, they were mistaken about their baptism, but the reference does show that John's fame had spread far and wide.[33] About this same time Apollos' arrival from Alexandria, "knowing only the baptism of John" (Acts 18:24-25), attests also to the spread of John the Baptist's influence into Egypt.

---

[33]A full discussion of these disciples at Ephesus is found in chapter five, dealing with the legality of John's baptism.

5

John and the Gospel of Jesus Christ

The previous chapter dealt with the circumstantial and historical events of John's public ministry; this chapter is concerned primarily with the content of John's preaching. An analysis of John's words leaves one impressed with his extensive knowledge of the gospel and the wide range of gospel topics which are found in his teachings.

Martin Luther felt that except for Jesus and Paul, John the Baptist was better informed on the Old Testament than any other personality in the New Testament.[34] On first observation, this great knowledge possessed by John is not immediately evident, but a careful reading of John's words reveals the depth of his understanding. Martin Luther was able to recognize the element of greatness and knowledge in John's teaching from the Bible as it occurs in our common versions; however, the Inspired Version by Joseph Smith projects an even greater image of John, especially with regard to the scope of his gospel knowledge.

The New Testament excerpts of John's utterances give scant attention to anything John may have said about the law of Moses or its accompanying ritual; yet he surely would have known of these things and observed them himself.[35] As we have previously mentioned, John

---

[34]"There was never any that understood the Old Testament so well as St. Paul, except John the Baptist." Thomas Kepler, ed., *The Table Talk of Martin Luther* (Cleveland: The World Publishing Company, 1952), p. 255.

[35]For example, the Nephite prophets observed the law of Moses, notwithstanding that they had also the gospel (2 Nephi 25:24).

came both as a *forerunner* to prepare the way before the Lord and also as a *witness* that Jesus is the Messiah, and what we have of John's teachings are directed primarily to these ends. To prepare the way before the Lord and bear a witness of him required that John have considerably more to say than simply to mention the fact that the Messiah was coming. He was divinely commissioned to "overthrow the kingdom of the Jews," and "prepare . . . [a people] for the coming of the Lord" (D&C 84:28). An adequate testimony must include something about the purpose of the Messiah's coming, the work that he would do, the significance of that work, and something of the laws and principles pertaining to his kingdom. If such were not the case, then what was the need of the pre-earth appointment of the fore-runner in the Grand Council of heaven, the frequent mention of him in prophecy, the specific earthly lineage, the special ordination by an angel, and the years of training and preparation prior to the fore-runner's public ministry? The responsibilities of John's divine com-mission included a proclamation of the laws and principles of the gospel as well as the announcement that the Messiah was among them in person.

The angel Gabriel's explanatory prediction of John's forthcoming earthly mission makes it evident that John would need remarkable preaching ability and a substantial amount of knowledge and com-prehension of the gospel. Among the things spoken by Gabriel about John are that

> he shall be great in the sight of the Lord, . . . and he shall be filled with the Holy Ghost. . . .
> And many of the children of Israel shall he turn to the Lord. . . .
> And he shall . . . turn . . . the disobedient to the wisdom of the just; to make ready a people prepared for the Lord. [Luke 1:15-17.]

In similar manner the blessing of Zacharias upon John, commonly called the Benedictus, foreshadows that John would have an accurate and extensive knowledge of the gospel. Said Zacharias:

> And thou, child, shalt be called the prophet of the Highest: for thou shalt go before the face of the Lord . . .
> To give knowledge of salvation unto his people . . . ,
> To give light to them that sit in darkness . . . , to guide our feet into the way of peace. [Luke 1:76-77, 79.]

Thus the mission of John was to be multi-purposive, and the suc-cessful execution of it would require that he be adequately prepared with knowledge, understanding, ability, and inspiration. The breadth of John's mission is emphasized in the Inspired Version in a number of passages, of which one extract is given below, with the corresponding passage from the King James Version included for comparison.

King James Version	Inspired Version
John 1:6 There was a man sent from God, whose name was John.	John 1:6 There was a man sent from God, whose name was John.
7 The same came for a witness, to bear witness of the Light, that all men through him might believe.	7 The same came into the world for a witness, to bear witness of the light, to bear *record of the gospel through the Son, unto all,* that through him *men* might believe.
8 He was not that Light, but was sent to bear witness of that Light.	8 He was not that light, but came to bear witness of that light,
9 That was the true Light, which lighteth every man that cometh into the world.	9 *Which* was the true light, which lighteth every man *who* cometh into the world.

Here the Inspired Version categorically declares that John came into the world "to bear record of the gospel through the Son" — a stronger and more descriptive statement than is given in the King James Version.

The doctrinal topics found in John's preaching are many, and a skeletal list is given below. Following the listing, the remainder of this chapter represents the texts from the various scriptural sources, accompanied by a discussion of each topic. Doctrinal topics taught by John include at least the following:

1. Repentance from sin
2. Baptism in water
3. Confession of sin
4. The nearness of the Kingdom
5. The objectives of Christ's ministry
   a. To take away the sins of the world
   b. To bring salvation to the heathen nations
   c. To gather scattered Israel
   d. To make possible the preaching of the gospel to the gentiles
   e. To be a light to those who sit in darkness
   f. To bring to pass the resurrection from the dead
6. The Lord's subsequent ascension to heaven, until the fulness of time
   a. When the Law and testimony shall be sealed
   b. When the keys of the kingdom shall be delivered unto the Father
7. The Second Coming of Christ
   a. A day of judgment

b. A day of justice
c. A day when the ungodly will be convinced of their sin
d. A day of power
e. A day when the mountains shall be brought down
f. A day when all flesh shall see the salvation of God
8. The law of gospel adoption
9. Judgment according to works
10. Brotherly kindness, honesty, and justice
11. The imminent advent of the Messiah
   a. To baptize with water
   b. To baptize with the Holy Ghost
12. The sign of the dove
13. Identification of Jesus as the Messiah, the Son of God
14. Jesus as the Lamb of God
15. The pre-mortal existence of Jesus
16. The spirit of Elias
   a. An Elias to be a forerunner
   b. An Elias to restore all things
17. Prayer
18. Fasting
19. Moral cleanliness
20. The divinity of Jesus Christ
   a. His coming from heaven
   b. His fulness of the spirit
   c. All things given into his hands

We will now discuss these items in as nearly the situational context as can be determined from the scriptures. Of course, each of these doctrines would no doubt be taught many times by John, but our discussion will follow the instances that are recorded in the scriptures.

Repentance, Baptism, and Confession

The records of Matthew, Mark, and Luke give an account of John's earliest preaching. Let us first consider the account in the third chapter of Matthew, comparing the Inspired Version and the King James Version.

King James Version	Inspired Version
1 In those days came John the Baptist preaching in the wilderness of Judaea,	27 And in those days came John the Baptist, preaching in the wilderness of Judea,
2 And saying, Repent ye: for the kingdom of heaven is at hand.	28 And saying, Repent ye: for the kingdom of heaven is at hand.

3 For this is he that was spoken of by the prophet Esaias, saying, The voice of one crying in the wilderness, Prepare ye the way of the Lord, make his paths straight. . . .

5 Then went out to him Jerusalem, and all Judaea, and all the region round about Jordan,

6 And were baptized of him in Jordan, confessing their sins.

29 For *I am* he *who* was spoken of by the prophet Esaias, saying, The voice of one crying in the wilderness, Prepare ye the way of the Lord and make his paths straight. . . .

31 Then went out to him Jerusalem, and all Judea, and all the region round about Jordan.

32 And many were baptized of him in Jordan, confessing their sins.

In the foregoing passage, verse two gives John's message as "Repent ye: for the kingdom of heaven is at hand." Verse three appears as commentary by Matthew in the King James Version, "For this is he that . . . ," but in the Inspired Version the same material is presented as John the Baptist himself quoting the words of the prophet Isaiah: "For *I am* he who . . ." Although Matthew's record at this point does not specifically say that John preached baptism, the accounts given by Mark and Luke do say that John was "preaching the baptism of repentance for the remission of sins" (Luke 3:3, also Mark 1:4). None of the records categorically state that John asked for confessions, but from the fact that when people came to be baptized of him they confessed their sins (Matthew 3:5-6) it is evident that he required it of them. Since confession of sin is an integral part of true repentance it is contained within the general area of repentance in John's preaching.

The Kingdom Is at Hand

As noted above, when John came preaching he announced, "The kingdom of heaven is at hand" (Matthew 3:2). We do not have much from John himself on this subject, but the Prophet Joseph Smith explained the import of John's preaching concerning the "kingdom" and defined John's relationship to that kingdom as follows:

As touching the Gospel and baptism that John preached, I would say that John came preaching the Gospel for the remission of sins; he had his authority from God, and the oracles of God were with him, and the kingdom of God for a season seemed to rest with John alone. The Lord promised Zacharias that he should have a son who was a descendant of Aaron, the Lord having promised that the priesthood should continue with Aaron and his seed throughout their generations. Let no man take this honor upon himself, except he be called of God, as was Aaron; and Aaron received his call by revelation. An angel of God also appeared unto Zacharias while in the Temple, and told him that he should have a son, whose name should be John, and he should be filled with the Holy Ghost. Zacharias was a priest of God, and officiating in the Temple, and John was a priest after his father, and held the keys of the Aaronic Priesthood, and was called of God to preach the Gospel of the kingdom of God. The Jews, as a nation, having departed from the law of God and the Gospel of the Lord, prepared the way for transferring it to the Gentiles.

But, says one, the kingdom of God could not be set up in the days of John, for John said the kingdom was at hand. But I would ask if it could be any nearer to them than to be in the hands of John. The people need not wait for the days of Pentecost to find the kingdom of God, for John had it with him, and he came forth from the wilderness crying out, "Repent ye, for the kingdom of heaven is nigh at hand," as much as to say, "Out here I have got the kingdom of God, and you can get it, and I am coming after you; and if you don't receive it, you will be damned;" and the scriptures represent that all Jerusalem went out unto John's baptism. There was a legal administrator, and those that were baptized were subjects for a king; and also the laws and oracles of God were there; therefore the kingdom of God was there; for no man could have better authority to administer than John; and our Savior submitted to that authority Himself, by being baptized by John; therefore the kingdom of God was set up on the earth, even in the days of John. . . .

There is a difference between the kingdom of God and the fruits and blessings that flow from the kingdom; because there were more miracles, gifts, visions, healings, tongues, &c., in the days of Jesus Christ and His apostles, and on the day of Pentecost, than under John's administration, it does not prove by any means that John had not the kingdom of God, any more than it would that a woman had not a milkpan because she had not a pan of milk, for while the pan might be compared to the kingdom, the milk might be compared to the blessings of the kingdom.

John was a priest after the order of Aaron, and had the keys of that priesthood, and came forth preaching repentance and baptism for the remission of sins, but at the same time cries out, "There cometh one mightier than I after me, the latchet of whose shoes I am not worthy to stoop down and unloose," and Christ came according to the words of John, and He was greater than John, because He held the keys of the Melchizedek Priesthood and kingdom of God, and had before revealed the priesthood of Moses, yet Christ was baptized by John to fulfill all righteousness. . . .

. . . It is evident the kingdom of God was on the earth, and John prepared subjects for the kingdom, by preaching the Gospel to them and baptizing them, and he prepared the way before the Savior, or came as a forerunner, and prepared subjects for the preaching of Christ; and Christ preached through Jerusalem on the same ground where John had preached; and when the apostles were raised up, they worked in Jerusalem, and Jesus commanded them to tarry there until they were endowed with power from on high. Had they not work to do in Jerusalem? They did work, and prepared a people for the Pentecost. The kingdom of God was with them before the day of Pentecost, as well as afterwards; and it was also with John, and he preached the same Gospel and baptism that Jesus and the apostles preached after him.[36]

Jesus also spoke of John's relationship to the kingdom. Because the Inspired Version gives a clear account it is included here in comparison with the King James Version of Matthew 11:12-13.

King James Version	Inspired Version
12 And from the days of John the Baptist until now the kingdom of heaven suffereth violence, and the violent take it by force.	12 And from the days of John the Baptist until now, the kingdom of heaven suffereth violence, and the violent take it by force.
13 For all the prophets and the law prophesied until John.	13 *But the days will come, when the violent shall have no power;* for all the prophets and the law prophesied *that it should be thus* until John.
	14 *Yea, as many as have prophesied have foretold of these days.*

The book of Luke (16:16) gives a somewhat different account, on which the Inspired Version elaborates considerably. The Lord's words are directed to the Pharisees:

King James Version	Inspired Version
16 The law and the prophets were until John: since that time the kingdom of God is preached, and every man presseth into it.	17 *Then said Jesus unto them,* The law and the prophets *testify of me; yea, and all the prophets who have written, even* until John, *have foretold of these days.*
	18 Since that time, the kingdom of God is preached, and every man *who seeketh truth* presseth into it. . . .
	21 . . . And you pervert the right way; and the kingdom of heaven suffereth violence of

---

[36]*Teachings*, pp. 272-74.

you; and you persecute the
meek; and in your violence you
seek to destroy the kingdom;
and ye take the children of the
kingdom by force.

The foregoing verses, especially from the Inspired Version, suggest
that the kingdom of God was on the earth in the days of John the
Baptist. On this matter the Prophet Joseph commented:

John held the Aaronic Priesthood and was a legal administrator, and
the forerunner of Christ, and came to prepare the way before him. . . .
The keys of the Aaronic Priesthood were committed unto him, and
he was as the voice of one crying in the wilderness saying: "Prepare ye
the way of the Lord and make his paths straight."
The Kingdom of heaven suffereth violence, etc.
The kingdom of heaven continueth in authority until John.
The authority taketh it by absolute power.
John having the power took the Kingdom by authority.
How have you obtained all this great knowledge? By the gift of the
Holy Ghost.
Wrested the Kingdom from the Jews.
Of these stony Gentiles — these dogs — to raise up children
unto Abraham.
The Savior said unto John, I must be baptized by you. Why so? To
fulfil all righteousness. John refuses at first, but afterwards obeyed
by administering the ordinance of baptism unto him, Jesus having no
other legal administrator to apply to.[37]

The Prophet's commentary makes these passages about John and the
kingdom much more meaningful to us, and hence serves also to en-
large our understanding of John's ministry. The Prophet's words
have particular bearing upon the statement in Doctrine and Covenants 84:28 that John was ordained "to overthrow the kingdom of
the Jews," which he did, setting up the kingdom of God in its stead.

A Preview of Christ's Ministry

When John came preaching and baptizing, he also declared that he
was doing so because he was the forerunner of the Messiah. But he
said it in grand style, and he gave a considerable explanation about
the Messiah's mission and kingdom. The Inspired Version offers the
fullest account, and in this particular instance is especially informa-
tive. The King James Version is included for comparison.

---

[37]Teachings, pp. 318-19.

King James Version

Luke 3:3 And he came into all the country about Jordan, preaching the baptism of repentance for the remission of sins;

4 As it is written in the book of the words of Esaias the prophet, saying, The voice of one crying in the wilderness, Prepare ye the way of the Lord, make his paths straight. .

5 Every valley shall be filled, and every mountain and hill

Inspired Version

Luke 3:3 And he came into all the country about Jordan, preaching the baptism of repentance for the remission of sins.

4 As it is written in the book *of the prophet* Esaias; *and these are the words,* saying, The voice of one crying in the wilderness, Prepare ye the way of the Lord, and make his paths straight.

5 For behold, and lo, he shall come, as it is written in the book of the prophets, to take away the sins of the world, and to bring salvation unto the heathen nations, to gather together those who are lost, who are of the sheepfold of Israel;

6 Yea, even the dispersed and afflicted; and also to prepare the way, and make possible the preaching of the gospel unto the Gentiles;

7 And to be a light unto all who sit in darkness, unto the uttermost parts of the earth; to bring to pass the resurrection from the dead, and to ascend up on high, to dwell on the right hand of the Father,

8 Until the fulness of time, and the law and the testimony shall be sealed, and the keys of the kingdom shall be delivered up again unto the Father;

9 To administer justice unto all; to come down in judgment upon all, and to convince all the ungodly of their ungodly deeds, which they have committed; and all this in the day that he shall come;

10 *For it is a day of power; yea,* every valley shall be filled, and

shall be brought low; and the crooked shall be made straight, and the rough ways shall be made smooth;	every mountain and hill shall be brought low; the crooked shall be made straight, and the rough ways made smooth;
6 And all flesh shall see the salvation of God.	11 And all flesh shall see the salvation of God.

This lengthy addition in the Inspired Version not only attests to John's extensive understanding of the Messiah and of the gospel, but it also corrects an erroneous impression which in the King James Version of Luke confuses the events of Christ's first and second comings. As given in the King James Version, Luke quotes from Isaiah, first relating the prophecy to John's mission and then citing events that are not fulfilled until the latter days, stating specifically that the mountains would be laid low and all flesh would see the salvation of God. The Inspired Version gives John, not Luke, as the one who quotes the Isaiah passage. John relates it to himself and clearly separates the events of the Messiah's first coming from those of his second coming. In making this distinct separation, John first gives several particulars about the precise purpose of the Messiah's earthly mission, of which John himself was the forerunner, and then describes events of a different nature at the second coming of Christ in the "fulness of time," which would be a day of power and of judgment. That both John and Luke correctly understood these things is evident from the Inspired Version, which offers the following particular doctrinal items of John's message at this point:

The Lord will come —

1. to take away the sins of the world;
2. to bring salvation to the heathen nations;
3. to gather scattered Israel;
4. to make possible the preaching of the gospel to the Gentiles;
5. to be a light to all who sit in darkness;
6. to bring to pass the resurrection from the dead.
7. The Lord will then ascend to the right hand of the Father on high,
8. until the fulness of time,
9. when the law and the testimony are sealed, and
10. the keys of the kingdom are delivered again to the father.
11. Then the Lord will come down in judgment upon all,
12. to administer justice unto all, and
13. to convince all the ungodly of their deeds.
14. For it is a day of power, when
15. the mountains shall be brought down and
16. all flesh shall see the salvation of God.

Not only is the foregoing an eloquent recitation of the Messiah's forthcoming mission, but it is substantially a comprehensive summary of the message of Isaiah as well. It is interesting to note how frequently the greatest doctrinal preachers were very familiar with Isaiah's writings. This is true of Nephi, Jacob, John the Baptist, Paul, and the Savior himself, each of whom quoted extensively from Isaiah's words.[38]

A Visit from the Pharisees and Sadducees

Returning to the account given by Matthew, we find the following encounter between John and the Pharisees and Sadducees:[39]

King James Version	Inspired Version
Matt. 3:7 But when he saw many of the Pharisees and Sadducees come to his baptism, he said unto them, O generation of vipers, who hath warned you to flee from the wrath to come?	Matt. 3:33 But when he saw many of the Pharisees and Sadducees come to his baptism, he said unto them, O, generation of vipers! who hath warned you to flee from the wrath to come?
	34 Why is it that ye receive not the preaching of him whom God hath sent? If ye receive not this in your hearts, ye receive not me; and if ye receive not me, ye receive not him of whom I am sent to bear record; and for your sins ye have no cloak.
8 Bring forth therefore fruits meet for repentance.	35 *Repent, therefore, and* bring forth fruits meet for repentance.

It is evident from the foregoing passage that those who came to hear John did not all come for the same reasons. Some came to hear a prophet, repent, confess their sins, and be baptized. The Pharisees generally came for other reasons. The additional material given in the Inspired Version (verse 34) suggests that the Pharisees and Sadducees had already made it plain that they were not sympathetic with John or his proclamation. Even more than simply being unsympathetic and indifferent, they had firmly rejected him; hence John's declaration, quoted above from the Inspired Version, that if they received not his teaching they received not him, and if they

---

[38]This particular quotation in Luke is consistent with Luke's general orientation, which is favorable to the gentiles. It is significant that this particular enlargement should appear in Luke (consistent with the gentile orientation of both Luke and Paul), rather than in Matthew, which is very pro-Jewish.

[39]Luke gives essentially the same passage but does not direct it specifically to the Pharisees and Sadducees.

received not him they received not him whom he represented. This prior rejection of John by the Jewish leaders also gives meaning to John's blunt query, "O generation of vipers! who hath warned you to flee from the wrath to come?" It is as if he said, "You have not accepted me or my message, so why have you come? Who, then, has warned you?"

Doubtless they had not come from any motive of repentance or desire to be baptized by John. They were probably curious to an extent, but it was a curiosity of a special sort. John was immensely popular. The common people were flocking to him as a prophet (Matthew 21:26). The religious leaders of Jerusalem would not sit idly by and let him make inroads into their flock. They would know more about this innovator. They had heard about him; now they would see and hear him for themselves. They might even have expected to trap him in his words, and confound him and openly embarrass him before all the people. After all, this man was not a graduate of the rabbinical schools, nor was he licensed by them to preach. Perhaps they had the same thoughts about John that they later had about Jesus when they asked, "How knoweth this man letters, having never learned?" (John 7:15), or in other words, "How could this man know enough to preach, having never attended our schools?" It is most likely that the Pharisees and Sadducees came to hear John not from curiosity alone but with a settled determination to obstruct him. As we shall see, the Sanhedrin itself later took notice and made an official inquiry concerning him.

The Law of Gospel Adoption

In continuing his rebuke of the Pharisees and Sadducees, John declared that their lineage from Father Abraham was not in itself sufficient for their salvation, and that God could raise up children unto Abraham from another source. The best account of the situation is found in the Inspired Version.

King James Version	Inspired Version
Matt. 3:9 And think not to say within yourselves, We have Abraham to our father: for I say unto you, that God is able of these stones to raise up children unto Abraham.	Matt. 3:36 And think not to say within yourselves, We *are the children of Abraham, and we only have power to bring seed unto our father Abraham;* for I say unto you that God is able of these stones to raise up children unto Abraham.

The account in Luke is similar:

King James Version	Inspired Version
Luke 3:8 . . . and begin not to say within yourselves, We have Abraham to our father: for I say unto you, That God is able of these stones to raise up children unto Abraham.	Luke 3:13 . . . and begin not to say within yourselves, *Abraham is our father; we have kept the commandments of God, and none can inherit the promises but the children of Abraham;* for I say unto you, That God is able of these stones to raise up children unto Abraham.

From these enlargements it is clear that John attacked the attitude of exclusiveness of the Pharisees and Sadducees who relied on their descent from Abraham and who believed that such a lineage guaranteed their inheritance of the promises and blessings of Abraham. Although they pretended to be righteous, their emphasis was on lineage rather than on righteousness. John's statement about God's ability to raise up children unto Abraham from the stones reveals that John understood the true basis of all gospel covenants. He realized that "the Lord esteemeth all flesh in one; [and only] he that is righteous is favored of God" (1 Nephi 17:35). Furthermore, he knew that eternal blessings are not obtained by inheritance alone. Since John understood this concept, it was a simple matter for him to explain to them that people not of Abraham's lineage (even the "stony" Gentiles[40]) could be adopted into the gospel covenant and thereby become heirs of the promises given to Abraham and be accounted as Abraham's seed.

The principle of adoption through the law of the gospel had been revealed and explained to Abraham himself, whereby he knew that as "father of the faithful" — as he is often called — he would be accounted the father of "as many as receive this Gospel" — not only those of the literal seed of his body, but also those who would receive the gospel who were not naturally of his lineage (Abraham 2:9-11), that is, from among the gentiles.

Some have taken a very literal interpretation of John's words and supposed he meant that God could raise up children from the very rocks and stones along the banks of the Jordan. However, such a view is not satisfactory in the light of the covenant of adoption which the Lord made with Abraham. John understood the nature of this covenant, but it seems that the Pharisees and Sadducees did not.

It is interesting to note that Paul also recognized this principle and taught it to the Romans (4:11) and the Galatians (3:28-29).

---

[40]*Teachings*, p. 319.

Judgment According to Works

John called upon the Pharisees and Sadducees to show evidence of repentance by bringing forth the fruit that is "meet for," or "worthy of" — or evidence of — repentance, and he warned them that by their works they would be judged. Said he:

> And now also the ax is laid unto the root of the trees: every tree therefore which bringeth not forth good fruit is hewn down, and cast into the fire. [Luke 3:9; also Matthew 3:10.]

The Inspired Version offers one change in the passage to improve the time element, consistent with the distinction, discussed earlier, between the different events pertaining to the first and the second comings of the Lord. Instead of saying "every tree . . . *is* hewn the Inspired Version reads "every tree . . . *shall be* hewn down" (Matthew 3:37; Luke 3:14).

Brotherly Kindness, Honesty, and Justice

Luke preserves some other items that show the depth of John's understanding and the scope of his subject matter. When the people heard John's stinging rebuke of the Pharisees and Sadducees, they came to him and said, "What shall we do *then?*" (Luke 3:15, I.V.). The word "then" points back to John's denunciation of the others, and shows that their coming to John was a direct result of his denunciation of the sophistry, self-righteousness, and hypocrisy of the Pharisees and Sadducees. Forcefulness and plainness in preaching are desirable qualities, and the vigor of John's words brought honest-hearted persons to inquire further. To them he answered, "He that hath two coats, let him impart to him that hath none; and he that hath meat, let him do likewise" (Luke 3:11).

When the publicans came to him and asked, "Master what shall we do?" he said, "Exact no more than that which is appointed you" (Luke 3:12-13). The Inspired Version gives an expanded account of this event:

King James Version	Inspired Version
Luke 3:12 Then came also publicans to be baptized, and said unto him, Master, what shall we do?	Luke 3:17 Then came also publicans to be baptized, and said unto him, Master, what shall we do?
13 And he said unto them, Exact no more than that which is appointed you.	18 And he said unto them, Exact no more than that which is appointed *unto* you.
	19 For it is well known unto

58

you, Theophilus, that after the manner of the Jews, and according to the custom of their law in receiving money into the treasury, that out of the abundance which was received, was appointed unto the poor, every man his portion;

20 And after this manner did the publicans also, wherefore John said unto them, Exact no more than that which is appointed you.

Verses 19 and 20 in the above extract from the Inspired Version are interesting for a number of reasons. First, they explain the Jewish custom of receiving monies for the poor, and also the means by which the publicans, or tax collectors, were able to collect more than was appointed and keep the difference for themselves. John deplored this form of extortion. Secondly, these verses attest to John's familiarity with the ways of men and with the social customs of his day, which in turn suggests that he hadn't spent his years of preparation as a lonely hermit away from all humanity. Thirdly, these verses are interesting in that they represent a personal note from Luke to his gentile friend Theophilus. Apparently Luke felt it necessary to explain matters of Jewish law and custom to a non-Jew.

Then came the soldiers also and inquired of John, asking what they should do. John's reply was that they should "do violence to no man, neither accuse any falsely; and be content with your wages" (Luke 3:14).

John Announces the Coming of the Messiah

So powerful was John's preaching that "the people were in expectation, and all men mused in their hearts of John, whether he were the Christ or not" (Luke 3:15). But John answered, saying unto them all:

I indeed baptize you with water; but one mightier than I cometh, the latchet of whose shoes I am not worthy to unloose: he shall baptize you with the Holy Ghost and with fire:

Whose fan is in his hand, and he will throughly purge his floor, and will gather the wheat into his garner; but the chaff he will burn with fire unquenchable. [Luke 3:16-17.]

The Inspired Version reads essentially the same as the King James Version of Luke at this point. John was careful to draw the strict distinction between himself and the Messiah, and between the things that he himself could do and what the Messiah would do. "I will baptize you with water," he said, in effect, "but when he of whom I bear witness comes, he will baptize you with the Holy Ghost and fire, for he is mightier than I." (See Matthew 3:38, I.V.)

John Predicts Jesus' Baptizing

A statement similar to the one just quoted occurs in Mark 1:7-8. We could pass over the Marcan passage with no further observation, if it were not for an important change that occurs in this passage in the Inspired Version.

King James Version	Inspired Version
Mark 1:7 . . . There cometh one mightier than I after me, the latchet of whose shoes I am not worthy to stoop down and unloose.	Mark 1:5 . . . There cometh one mightier than I after me, the latchet of whose shoes I am not worthy to stoop down and unloose.
8 I indeed have baptized you with water: but he shall baptize you with the Holy Ghost.	6 I indeed have baptized you with water; but he shall *not only baptize you with water, but with fire,* and the Holy Ghost.

The important element here is that Jesus is to perform baptisms with water. This matter has often been debated in the world of biblical scholarship, usually with the decision that Jesus did not perform water baptisms. Such a conclusion is reached by the incorrect rendition of John 4:2 in the King James Version, which reads: "Though Jesus himself baptized not, but his disciples" (John 4:2). This is ambiguous even so, and contradicts an earlier statement in John 3:22 that Jesus "tarried with . . . [his disciples] and baptized."

The Inspired Version, however, corrects the false inference of John 4:2 to read, "though he himself baptized not so many as his disciples; For he suffered them for an example, preferring one another" (John 4:3-4 I.V.). The Inspired Version is explicit on this matter, and contains still another reference to Jesus performing water baptisms. John 1:28 (I.V.) represents the Baptist as saying, "He [the Lamb of God] shall baptize, not only with water, but with fire, and with the Holy Ghost." This passage, given as the words of John the Baptist, is discussed later, but is quoted at this point for sake of clarity.

The Sign of the Dove

Very soon after John baptized Jesus he saw the heavens open and beheld the Holy Ghost in the sign of a dove descend upon Jesus. Just how soon this happened after the baptism of Jesus we do not know. The records of Matthew and Mark imply that it happened as Jesus came "straightway" out of the water, and thus give the impression of immediacy. As a result, the event is often portrayed in works of art as occurring while Jesus was just emerging from the water. Luke's account, however, is slightly different, suggesting that the Holy Ghost descended while Jesus was praying after he was baptized. This is probably the most realistic picture, and allows for at least a few moments to have elapsed.

The manner in which the account is given in Matthew, Mark, and Luke leaves the reader uncertain whether it was Jesus only or both he and John who saw the heavens open and witnessed the Holy Ghost descend. It is made clear, however, in the Inspired Version that John indeed witnessed the miraculous event:

King James Version	Inspired Version
Matt. 3:16 And Jesus, when he was baptized went up straight-way out of the water: and, lo, the heavens were opened unto him, and he saw the Spirit of God descending like a dove, and lighting upon him:	Matt. 3:45 And Jesus when he was baptized, went up straight-way out of the water; *and John saw*, and lo, the heavens were opened unto him, and he saw the Spirit of God descending like a dove and lighting upon *Jesus.*
17 And lo a voice from heaven, saying, This is my beloved Son, in whom I am well pleased.	46 And lo, *he heard* a voice from heaven, saying, This is my beloved Son, in whom I am well pleased. *Hear ye him.*

The effect of the Inspired Version is to harmonize the account in Matthew with John's own testimony, which he gave at a later date and which is recorded in John 1:29-34. As we learn from the source, it was altogether necessary that John be a witness of the Holy Ghost descending upon Jesus, since it was a prearranged sign by which he was to know that he had baptized the Messiah. John's explanation of this matter was given after he had baptized Jesus and at a time when he identified Jesus as the Messiah then standing among them.

While Jesus was in the wilderness John continued to preach and baptize. About this time the Sanhedrin sent a delegation of priests and Levites (consisting mostly of Pharisees) to ask him who he was — if he was Elias, or even, perhaps, the prophet (Messiah) who Moses had said would come (John 1:19-22). John did not deny that he was Elias, but carefully explained that he was not the Elias who would restore all things, or the Messiah, but was the one to prepare the way and bear witness of the Messiah, who was then among them but whom they did not know. He was not even worthy, he said, to unloose the latchet of the Messiah's shoes, for the Messiah, although coming after him, was preferred before him (John 1:23-27).

The "next day" John saw Jesus — who had probably just returned from forty days in the wilderness — coming to him, and he announced: "Behold the Lamb of God, which taketh away the sin of the world" (John 1:29).

John then explained that Jesus was the man whom he (John) had been sent to baptize and to bear record of, and that this was indeed the "Son of God" (John 1:30-34). He had not personally known Jesus, he said, but had known only that the Messiah *was* to be made manifest, and that he would be able to identify Jesus as the Messiah by the descent of the Holy Ghost in the sign of a dove. At this point the Inspired Version and the King James Version read somewhat differently:

King James Version	Inspired Version
John 1:29 The next day John seeth Jesus coming unto him, and saith, Behold the Lamb of God, which taketh away the sin of the world.	John 1:29 The next day John seeth Jesus coming unto him, and said; Behold the Lamb of God, who taketh away the sin of the world!
30 This is he of whom I said, After me cometh a man which is preferred before me: for he was before me.	30 And John bare record of him unto the people, saying, This is he of whom I said; After me cometh a man who is preferred before me; for he was before me,
31 And I knew him not: but that he should be made manifest to Israel, therefore am I come baptizing with water.	and I knew him, *and* that he should be made manifest to Israel; therefore am I come baptizing with water.
32 And John bare record, saying, I saw the Spirit descending from heaven like a dove, and it abode upon him.	31 And John bare record, saying; *When he was baptized of me,* I saw the Spirit descending from heaven like a dove, and it abode upon him.
33 And I knew him not: but he that sent me to baptize with water, the same said unto me, Upon whom thou shalt see the Spirit descending, and remaining on him, the same is he which baptizeth with the Holy Ghost.	32 And I *knew him;* for he who sent me to baptize with water, the same said unto me; Upon whom thou shalt see the Spirit descending, and remaining on him, the same is he who baptizeth with the Holy Ghost.
34 And I saw, and bare record that this is the Son of God.	33 And I saw, and bare record that this is the Son of God.

The essential difference between these two accounts hinges on whether John "knew him" or "knew him not." The difference isn't serious and is more apparent than real. In the King James Version John is represented as saying that he did not know Jesus until he baptized him and saw the Holy Ghost descend upon him, and then he knew that this was the Son of God. In the Inspired Version John is saying that he knew exactly who Jesus was, because he had baptized him and had seen the Spirit descend like a dove upon him, according to the predetermined sign for identification. In this respect there seems to be but scant difference between the King James Version and the Inspired Version in handling the fundamental meaning of the passage. There are, however, other considerations inherent in the passage that tend to favor the reading given in the Inspired Version. The interpretation depends on how much value is attached to the word "knew." Representing John as saying he "knew him not" implies that John did not know who the Messiah was, his mission, his divinity, and so forth. The words could be taken to mean more than simply not knowing Jesus personally, by sight and appearance. A statement of this nature, however, would not be in harmony with John's total preaching, wherein he had vigorously announced that the Messiah would come and would baptize with the Holy Ghost and would be a judge, a refiner, and so forth. That John did not know Jesus personally as a man, though, is quite likely.

Furthermore, as described in chapter four, the account of John's ministry found in Matthew, Mark, and Luke deals with the period *before* he baptized Jesus, whereas the fourth Gospel deals with John's testimony *after* he had baptized Jesus. Because of this difference in time sequence, the rendering of the Inspired Version, which says John knew him because he had already baptized him, is more consistent with the post-baptism period than is the phraseology of the King James Version, which says "he knew him not." If this particular statement by John were in Matthew, Mark, or Luke, there would not have been so strong a need for a correction by the Prophet, but since it is in the fourth Gospel the wording of the Inspired Version achieves a greater consistency with the time period of the fourth Gospel.

Some may see a relationship between John's declaration that he did (or did not) know Jesus and the question of whether John and Jesus had met as children, particularly at the passover at age twelve. However, even if they did meet as beardless boys of twelve, there is no assurance that John would recognize Jesus eighteen years later when he had become a mature man. The sons of Jacob, for instance, did not recognize their younger brother Joseph when they met him in Egypt after a separation of many years and after he had grown to maturity, even though he probably did not have a beard (Genesis 42:7-8; 41:14).

A question is raised also why John, if he did *not* know Jesus, hesitated to baptize him and said, "I have need to be baptized of thee, and comest thou to me?" (Matthew 3:14). This episode, therefore, may argue for the proposition that John did know Jesus, and advocates thereof may glean support from the Inspired Version of John 1:29-34, as discussed above. On the other hand, it is very probable that John's fine spiritual sensibilities responded to the meekness and lowliness of Jesus and he was made aware of Jesus' native purity and moral dignity. When contrasted with John's own earthiness, great as he was, Jesus' greater spirituality might well have led John to exclaim that he ought to be baptized of Jesus.[41]

John's testimony concerning the sign of the dove was given in a revelation to Joseph Smith identified as Doctrine and Covenants 93:15:

> And I, John, bear record, and lo, the heavens were opened, and the Holy Ghost descended upon him in the form of a dove, and sat upon him, and there came a voice out of heaven saying: This is my beloved Son.

There was thus a manifestation of all three personages of the Godhead, the Father, the Son, and the Holy Ghost, and John had visual and audial contact with them. Although John had many visions and revelations, this event would be a major spiritual experience of his mortal life as well as one of the great events in the history of mankind. John was indeed a witness, of the highest order, to the divinity of the Messiah, to the reality of God, and to the importance of the events that were taking place. This gave John a sort of apostolic calling — not in the ordained sense, but in the sense of having a perfect knowledge of Christ, of being a witness for him, and of having heard the Father's voice declaring Jesus to be the Son of God.

The manifestation of the Holy Ghost in the sign of a dove is a phenomenon of special significance. The importance of the matter is suggested by the fact that it is mentioned so frequently in the scriptures. From Facsimile no. 2, item no. 7, of the Book of Abraham we learn that the sign of the dove as a token of the Holy Ghost was revealed to Abraham about eighteen hundred years before Christ. Six hundred years before the time of Christ, Nephi beheld in vision the Holy Ghost descending upon Jesus in the sign of a dove (1 Nephi 11:27; 2 Nephi 31:8). It is mentioned by Matthew, Mark, and Luke, and was declared by John to be the specific evidence to him that he had

---

[41]This is the view taken by James E. Talmage, *Jesus the Christ*, pp. 125-26.

baptized the Messiah (John 1:33). The matter is also recorded in the revelation now identified as Doctrine and Covenants 93:15, quoted just previously. The Prophet Joseph Smith discussed the antiquity and significance of this principle as follows:

> The sign of the dove was instituted before the creation of the world, a witness for the Holy Ghost, and the devil cannot come in the sign of a dove. The Holy Ghost is a personage, and is in the form of a personage. It does not confine itself to the *form* of the dove, but in the *sign* of the dove. The Holy Ghost cannot be transformed into a dove; but the sign of a dove was given to John to signify the truth of the deed, as the dove is an emblem or token of truth and innocence.[42]

One can only imagine the spiritual experience that engulfed John when he led the Son of God into the baptism waters and afterward beheld these celestial manifestations.

There were probably many people in the approximate area when John baptized Jesus. Would anyone besides John and Jesus have seen the Holy Ghost descend upon Jesus or hear the voice of the Father? Probably not. These manifestations were for John and Jesus alone, and it is likely that others standing nearby would not be accorded such a great privilege.

John Identifies Jesus as the Messiah and Son of God

Since the purpose of the sign of a dove was to testify of Jesus' messiahship, the passages that describe that phenomenon also tell of John identifying Jesus as the Messiah and Son of God. Having seen the sign, John boldly announced to the people that the Messiah was then standing among them but that they did not know him. He then went a step further and proceeded to point out Jesus in person to them and identified him as the Messiah (John 1:19-34).

John Teaches of the Atonement

Closely associated with John's identification of Jesus as the Messiah is his declaration that Jesus is the "Lamb of God, which taketh away the sin of the world" (John 1:29). In referring to Jesus by this title, John showed that he understood the mission of Jesus as the Redeemer, and as the Great Sacrifice who would shed his blood for the world. The blood sacrifices offered by patriarchs, prophets, and priests since the days of Adam were symbolic of the sacrifice that the Eternal Father would make of his Son. Every man sacrificed a lamb, but Jesus was the Lamb of God. It was necessary that John, as a priest of the Aaronic order, understand this important aspect of Jesus' forthcoming atonement.

---

[42]*Teachings*, p. 276.

John Teaches of Jesus' Premortal Existence

In John 1:15 it is recorded:

John bare witness of him, and cried, saying, This was he of whom I spake, He that cometh after me is preferred before me: for he was before me.

To the delegation from the Sanhedrin John said:

I baptize with water: but there standeth one among you, whom ye know not;

He it is, who coming after me is preferred before me, whose shoe's latchet I am not worthy to unloose. [John 1:26-27.]

And the next day following, seeing Jesus come to him, John said to the people:

This is he of whom I said, After me cometh a man which is preferred before me: for he was before me. [John 1:30.]

John was six months older than Jesus in mortality, but these passages illustrate that John knew that Jesus was in some sense before, or older than, he. This is intelligible only in terms of a premortal existence. In chapter six of this book we shall discuss John the Baptist's written record. Depending on one's view of the content of that record, it is possible to propose that John the Baptist also had a knowledge of Jesus' being the creator of the world, as recorded in John 1:1-14. On this basis, John the Baptist's knowledge and testimony of the premortal activities of Jesus would be much more extensive than we have ordinarily and traditionally supposed.

The Spirit of Elias

The angel Gabriel told Zacharias that John would go forth in "the spirit and power of Elias . . . to make ready a people prepared for the Lord" (Luke 1:17). Joseph the Prophet explained that "the spirit of Elias is to prepare the way for a greater revelation of God. . . . And when God sends a man into the world to prepare for a greater work, holding the keys of the power of Elias, it was called the doctrine of Elias, even from the early ages of the world."[43] This was the case with John the Baptist. The Prophet continued:

[John the Baptist] came crying through the wilderness, "Prepare ye the way of the Lord, make his paths straight." And they were informed, if they could receive it, it was the spirit of Elias; and John was

---

[43]*Teachings*, pp. 335-36.

very particular to tell the people, he was not that Light, but was sent to bear witness of that Light.

He told the people that his mission was to preach repentance and baptize with water; but it was He that should come after him that should baptize with fire and the Holy Ghost.

If he had been an impostor, he might have gone to work beyond his bounds, and undertook to have performed ordinances which did not belong to that office and calling, under the spirit of Elias. . . .

John did not transcend his bounds, but faithfully performed that part belonging to his office.[44]

Elias is both a personal name and a title or office.

We are informed by the Prophet Joseph Smith that Gabriel is Noah.[45] Luke says that it was Gabriel who visited Zacharias and gave him the promise of a son and explained that the son would go forth "in the spirit and power of Elias" as a forerunner to prepare the way before the Lord (Luke 1:17). However, in a revelation to the Prophet Joseph Smith it is said that it was "Elias" who came to Zacharias (D&C 27:7) and gave promise of a son. We can conclude, then, that the man Elias is the same individual as Noah or Gabriel.[46]

The subject becomes somewhat more complicated, however, because the word "Elias" is the Greek form of the Hebrew "Elijah"; hence the New Testament name for Elijah the prophet is translated "Elias." This is the case in James 5:17-18 and Luke 9:54, which refer to Elijah the prophet, and are not to be confused with the man Elias or with the spirit or office of Elias.

The word "Elias" occurs several times in the New Testament, with reference sometimes to the prophet Elijah and sometimes to the spirit, power, and office of Elias. The distinction is not made clear in the King James Version but is easier to follow in the Inspired Version, which also differentiates between an Elias who was to be a forerunner of Jesus and another Elias who was to restore all things. Because this distinction is not clear in the biblical texts used by the world, commentators often conclude erroneously that John the Baptist went forth in the spirit and power of Elijah. They have likewise coined a phrase or explanation to the effect that John, although not the "person of Elijah," was the "Elijah of prophecy" spoken of by Malachi (4:5-6), who would come before the great and dreadful day of the Lord. Consequently, many commentators have confused the ministry of John the Baptist in the meridian of time with the personal manifestations of the prophet Elijah before the second coming of the

[44]*Teachings*, pp. 335-36.
[45]*Teachings*, p. 157.
[46]See Smith, *Answers to Gospel Questions*, 3:138-41.

Lord in the fulness of times, and they have not understood the difference.

An Elias to Restore All Things

It is evident from the Inspired Version that John the Baptist understood his own situation relative to the office and calling of Elias. Soon after John baptized Jesus, and probably while Jesus was in the wilderness to fast and commune with God, the Jews sent a delegation of priests and Levites of the Pharisees to John to question him. (The term "Jews" here must be understood to mean the leaders of the Jews and probably has reference to the Sanhedrin.) The Pharisees and Sadducees had gone to hear John preach on an earlier occasion. Then they had gone privately, perhaps partly out of curiosity and partly out of disdain and disapproval of John. But this later time they came as official emissaries of the religious and civil leaders of Jewry. The mighty Sanhedrin itself had taken notice of John.

When the delegation from the Sanhedrin came to John at Bethabara beyond Jordan (John 1:28), they asked him who he thought he was and why he was baptizing, and if he was Elias, or perhaps the Prophet of whom Moses spoke, that is, the Christ. He explained that he was not the Christ or the Elias who was to restore all things, but he did not deny that he was an "Elias." He said he was "the voice of one crying in the wilderness," spoken of by Isaiah. The entire passage comparing the Inspired Version with the King James Version follows:

King James Version	Inspired Version
John 1:19 And this is the record of John, when the Jews sent priests and Levites from Jerusalem to ask him, Who art thou?	John 1:20 And this is the record of John, when the Jews sent priests and Levites from Jerusalem, to ask him; Who art thou?
20 And he confessed, and denied not; but confessed, I am not the Christ.	21 And he confessed, and denied not *that he was Elias;* but confessed, saying; I am not the Christ.
21 And they asked him, What then? Art thou Elias? And he saith, I am not. Art thou that prophet? And he answered, No.	22 Then said they unto him, *How* then art thou Elias? And he said, I am not *that Elias who was to restore all things.* And they asked him, saying, Art thou that prophet? And he answered, No.
22 Then said they unto him, Who art thou? that we may give an answer to them that sent us.	23 Then said they unto him, Who art thou? that we may give an answer to them that sent us.

What sayest thou of thyself?

23 He said, I am the voice of one crying in the wilderness, Make straight the way of the Lord, as said the prophet Esaias.

24 And they which were sent were of the Pharisees.

25 And they asked him, and said unto him, Why baptizest thou then, if thou be not that Christ, nor Elias, neither that prophet?

26 John answered them, saying, I baptize with water: but there standeth one among you, whom ye know not;

27 He it is, who coming after me is preferred before me, whose shoe's latchet I am not worthy to unloose.

What sayest thou of thyself?

24 He said, I am the voice of one crying in the wilderness, Make straight the way of the Lord, as saith the prophet Esaias.

25 And they who were sent were of the Pharisees.

26 And they asked him, and said unto him; Why baptizest thou then, if thou be not *the* Christ, nor Elias *who was to restore all things*, neither that prophet?

27 John answered them, saying; I baptize with water, but there standeth one among you, whom ye know not;

28 He it is *of whom I bear record. He is that prophet, even Elias*, who, coming after me, is preferred before me, whose shoe's latchet I am not worthy to unloose, *or whose place I am not able to fill; for he shall baptize, not only with water, but with fire, and with the Holy Ghost.*

The Jews apparently knew of some ancient prophecy of the scriptures which we do not have, that told of an Elias who would come and restore all things, and to this prophecy the delegation apparently referred when they asked John if he was Elias (verses 21-22, I.V.). He replied that he was an Elias, but not the Elias to restore all things. This same ancient prophecy, or combination of prophecies, apparently also inferred that *the* Elias who would restore all things would perform baptisms in water and also of the Holy Ghost.

The same prophecies also declared that the Christ would perform both kinds of baptisms. Therefore, the Jews asked John, "Why baptizest thou then, if thou be not the Christ, nor Elias who was to restore all things" (John 1:26, I.V.). John explained that he baptized with water *only*, and not with the Holy Ghost, and therefore could not qualify as the fulfillment of the ancient prophecy. But he pointed out to them that the one of whom he had borne witness was the promised Messiah, who would baptize with both water and the Holy Ghost (John 1:28, I.V.). Since the Jews did not understand that the Elias who would "restore all things," the prophet of whom Moses spoke, and the Christ were all the same person, John identified that relationship for them:

> He it is of whom I bear record. He is that prophet, even Elias, who, coming after me, is preferred before me, whose shoe's latchet I am not worthy to unloose, or whose place I am not able to fill; for he shall baptize, not only with water, but with fire, and with the Holy Ghost. [John 1:28, I.V.]

Since we today do not have this ancient prophecy with which both the Jews and John seemed to be familiar, we would not be able to untangle the statements in the New Testament about Elias if we did not have the help of the Inspired Version.

Later, when John was in prison, Jesus spoke to the multitude about him and said, "And if ye will receive it, this is Elias, which was for to come" (Matthew 11:14). The Inspired Version adds the clarifying comment: "And if ye will receive it, *verily, he was the* Elias, *who* was for to come *and prepare all things*" (Matthew 11:15).

Still later, after John was dead, Moses and Elias (Elijah) appeared with Jesus and three of the Twelve on the Mount of Transfiguration. Afterward, as Jesus and the three disciples were discussing the events that took place on the mount and also the yet future resurrection of Jesus, the disciples raised a question concerning "Elias." The discussion is presented more clearly in the Inspired Version than in the King James Version:

King James Version	Inspired Version
Matt. 17:10 And his disciples asked him, saying, Why then say the scribes that Elias must first come?	Matt. 17:9 And his disciples asked him, saying, Why then say the Scribes that Elias must first come?
11 And Jesus answered and said unto them, Elias truly shall first come, and restore all things.	10 And Jesus answered and said unto them, Elias truly shall first come, and restore all things, *as the prophets have written.*
12 But I say unto you, That Elias is come already, and they knew him not, but have done unto him whatsoever they listed. Likewise shall also the Son of man suffer of them.	11 *And again* I say unto you that Elias *has* come already, *concerning whom it is written, Behold, I will send my messenger, and he shall prepare the way before me; and they knew him not, and* have done unto him, whatsoever they listed.
	12 Likewise shall also the Son of Man suffer of them.
	13 *But I say unto you, Who is*

70

Elias? Behold, this is Elias, whom I send to prepare the way before me.

13 Then the disciples understood that he spake unto them of John the Baptist.

14 Then the disciples understood that he spake unto them of John the Baptist, *and also of another who should come and restore all things, as it is written by the prophets.*

The rendition of the Inspired Version clearly separates Elias the preparer from Elias the restorer, and identifies John the Baptist as the preparer and the one of whom Malachi spoke.

Mark's account of the discussion concerning Elias is similar to that given by Matthew, but differs in two significant points. One point of difference has to do with a statement that Elias the preparer has been rejected, "as it is written of him." Just *where* this is written is not stated, but the implication is that it is written in the Jewish scriptures, or, as we would call them, the Old Testament. There is no such scripture recognizable in our present Old Testament, but apparently the people of that day knew of such a writing. It may be part of the "Elias" prophecy referred to by the Pharisees when they came to John and perhaps also part of the "Elias" prophecy that the disciples asked Jesus about, both of which we have discussed in the preceding pages. The whole subject of Elias is clearer in the Inspired Version:

King James Version

Mark 9:11 And they asked him, saying, Why say the scribes that Elias must first come?

12 And he answered and told them, Elias verily cometh first, and restoreth all things; and how it is written of the Son of man, that he must suffer many things, and be set at nought.

13 But I say unto you, That Elias is indeed come, and they have done unto him whatsoever they listed, as it is written of him.

Inspired Version

Mark 9:9 And they asked him, saying, Why say the scribes that Elias must first come?

10 And he answered and told them, *saying,* Elias verily cometh first, *and prepareth* all things; and *teacheth you of the prophets;* how it is written of the Son of Man, that he must suffer many things, and be set at naught.

11 *Again* I say unto you, That Elias is indeed come, *but* they have done unto him whatsoever they listed; *and even* as it is written of him; *and he bore record of me, and they received him not. Verily this was Elias.*

The second point of difference in which Mark's account is unique has to do with the identification (in the Inspired Version) of John the Baptist as an Elias who was with Moses on the Mount of Transfiguration:

King James Version	Inspired Version
Mark 9:4 And there appeared unto them Elias with Moses: and they were talking with Jesus.	Mark 9:3 And there appeared unto them Elias with Moses, *or in other words, John the Baptist and Moses;* and they were talking with Jesus.[47]

It is most uncommon to think of John the Baptist in this manner, and the Inspired Version is almost confusing at this point. Since this was after John's death, but before the resurrection, John could be there as a spirit being only. What purpose he could serve is not known. We are informed in the Doctrine and Covenants that we have only a partial account of the events that transpired on the mount (D&C 63:20-21), and it may be that many holy beings were present, in addition to Elijah and Moses. Pres. Bruce R. McConkie suggests one reason for John's presence on the mount:

> It is not to be understood that John the Baptist was the Elias who appeared with Moses to confer keys and authority upon those who then held the Melchizedek Priesthood, which higher priesthood already embraced and included all of the authority and power John had held and exercised during his ministry. Rather, for some reason that remains unknown — because of the partial record of the proceedings — John played some other part in the glorious manifestations then vouchsafed to mortals. Perhaps he was there, as the last legal administrator under the Old Covenant, to symbolize that the law was fulfilled and all old things were done away, thus contrasting his position with that of Peter, James, and John who were then becoming the "first" legal administrators of the New Kingdom.[48]

It is abundantly clear that we do not yet have the full corpus of scripture and prophecy regarding the mission and calling of Elias and all that is involved therein, which was had by various people of the past, but with the aid of the Prophet Joseph's teachings and the Inspired Version of the Bible we can understand something of the nature of the calling of Elias and can find meaning in New Testament passages that otherwise would be misleading and/or obscure.

---

[47] I have examined the original manuscripts of the Inspired Version. The printed editions accurately represent the original handwritten notes for the passage in question, Mark 9:3.

[48] *Doctrinal New Testament Commentary,* 1: 404.

It is also certain that John the Baptist understood the matter perfectly and was able to explain all things pertaining to his own position and also that of the Messiah with relation to the doctrine of Elias — not only concerning an Elias to prepare the way but also concerning an Elias to restore all things.

John Teaches His Disciples to Pray

We do not have a specific incident in the ministry of John to which we may look for his teachings about prayer, and it is only indirectly that we learn of it. On one occasion, when Jesus had just finished a prayer, one of his disciples said unto him, "Lord, teach us to pray, as John also taught his disciples" (Luke 11:1). This single reference is all that we have relating to the subject.

John Teaches His Disciples to Fast

As in the case of John's teaching about prayer, we also have no direct word from John about the matter of fasting but learn of it from a statement of his disciples. Even so, it is not explicitly said that John taught his disciples to fast; it does seem, however, to be implied in the context of the situation. The references to the subject are found in Matthew 9:14, Mark 2:18, and Luke 5:33. These all give approximately the same account with a little variation, leaving it unclear whether it was John's disciples or the Pharisees who asked the question about fasting. In either case, the statement maintains that the disciples of John practiced fasting. The Inspired Version somewhat alters the account in Matthew and Mark but does not affect the point under consideration. Matthew tells us that John's disciples came to Jesus and asked, "Why do we and the Pharisees fast oft, but thy disciples fast not?" (Matthew 9:14). The question implies that John had taught his disciples to fast, and it also reveals that there was at least occasional contact and discussion between John's disciples and the disciples of Jesus. Otherwise, how could they make the comparison? The Lord's reply was:

> Can the children of the bridechamber mourn, as long as the bridegroom is with them? but the days will come, when the bridegroom shall be taken from them, and then shall they fast. [Matthew 9:15.]

John Teaches Moral Cleanliness

When Herod Antipas married Herodias, his brother Philip's wife, John told Herod, "It is not lawful for thee to have her" (Matthew 14: 3-4). John's vigor in defining moral cleanliness angered both Herod and Herodias and was contributory to his execution.

John Teaches of the Divinity of Jesus Christ

Towards the end of John's active public ministry, while he was baptizing at Aenon near Salim, we find the following:

King James Version	Inspired Version
John 3:25 Then there arose a question between some of John's disciples and the Jews about purifying.	John 3:26 Then there arose a question between some of John's disciples, and the Jews, about purifying.
26 And they came unto John, and said unto him, Rabbi, he that was with thee beyond Jordan, to whom thou barest witness, behold, the same baptizeth, and all men come to him.	27 And they came unto John, and said unto him, Rabbi, he *who* was with thee beyond Jordan, to whom thou bearest witness, behold, the same baptizeth, and *he receiveth of all people who* come *unto* him.

In this passage there are three related factors: first, the subject of purifying; second, the fact that Jesus baptized; and, third, the growing numbers of Jesus' disciples. The latter point is emphasized in the Inspired Version.

The first two issues are especially closely related. The subject of baptism was evidently involved in the controversy about purifying, and there is a suggestion that the disciples of John did not fully understand the purpose of the baptism performed by Jesus. So they came to John to ask him about it.

The major Jewish sects of that day seemingly did not practice baptism as an essential rite for themselves (although the people of the Dead Sea Scrolls apparently did) but required it for the cleansing of gentile proselytes to Judaism. Since John and Jesus both required even the Jews to be baptized for the remission of sins, this may have given rise to the question of purifying as related to baptism. Whether the "Jew" in the episode had it in mind or not we do not know, but it is clear that the disciples of John were making a comparison of the relative merits of John's baptism and Jesus' baptism. The Jew may have been comparing only the purpose of the Jewish-type baptism with John's baptism. However, if the Jew was arguing the differences between Jesus' baptism and John's baptism, it follows that he was acquainted with Jesus' teaching and might even have been a baptized disciple. All of these possibilities and probabilities are compatible with the facts of the case as given in verses 25 and 26, quoted above. Because of the particular frame of mind of his disciples, John's reply deals vigorously not so much with the particulars as with the fundamental status of Jesus as the Son of God and of John's own comparatively inferior position.

The third issue, that Jesus received all who came to him, is couched in a feeling of resentment on the part of John's disciples, who were jealous for John's own position and who observed that Jesus was making many converts. What was even worse, many of John's own disciples were leaving him and following Jesus. This was a point of major concern to John's disciples when they put the issue about "purifying" before him. John sensed this concern, and his answer is directed more to this point, since it is the most basic, than to the specific question of purifying. John bore a direct testimony to his disciples about the divinity of Christ, his own inferior relationship to Christ, and the necessity of men's accepting Jesus as the Son of God if they wished to have the fulness of eternal life. The passage, in John 3, is clearer in the Inspired Version:

King James Version	Inspired Version
27 John answered and said, A man can receive nothing, except it be given him from heaven.	28 John answered and said, A man can receive nothing, except it be given him from heaven.
28 Ye yourselves bear me witness, that I said, I am not the Christ, but that I am sent before him.	29 Ye yourselves bear me witness that I said, I am not the Christ, but that I am sent before him.
29 He that hath the bride is the bridegroom: but the friend of the bridegroom, which standeth and heareth him, rejoiceth greatly because of the bridegroom's voice: this my joy therefore is fulfilled.	30 He *who* hath the bride, is the bridegroom; but the friend of the bridegroom, *who* standeth and heareth him, rejoiceth greatly because of the bridegroom's voice; this my joy therefore is fulfilled.
30 He must increase, but I must decrease.	31 He must increase, but I must decrease.
31 He that cometh from above is above all: he that is of the earth is earthly, and speaketh of the earth: he that cometh from heaven is above all.	32 He *who* cometh from above is above all; he *who* is of the earth is earthly, and speaketh of the earth; he who cometh from heaven is above all. And what he hath seen and heard, that he testifieth; and *but few men* receive his testimony.
32 And what he hath seen and heard, that he testifieth; and no man receiveth his testimony.	
33 He that hath received his testimony hath set to his seal that God is true.	33 He who hath received his testimony, hath set to his seal that God is true.
34 For he whom God hath sent speaketh the words of God: for	34 For he whom God hath sent, speaketh the words of God; for

75

God giveth not the Spirit by measure unto him.	God giveth him not the Spirit by measure, *for he dwelleth in him, even the fulness.*
35 The Father loveth the Son, and hath given all things into his hand.	35 The Father loveth the Son, and hath given all things into his hands.
36 He that believeth on the Son hath everlasting life: and he that believeth not the Son shall not see life; but the wrath of God abideth on him.	36 And he who believeth on the Son hath everlasting life; *and shall receive of his fulness. But* he *who* believeth not the Son, *shall not receive of his fulness;* for the wrath of God *is* upon him.

Many commentators believe that the words of John the Baptist end with verse 30 in the King James Version and that verses 31 through 36 are the words of John the Beloved as he reflected on the status of Jesus while writing the Gospel record. This is discussed at length in chapter six of this work.

The Legality of John's Baptism

When the disciples left John and followed Jesus they did not need to be rebaptized, since John's baptism was sufficient. This was the view of the Prophet Joseph Smith:

John's mission was limited to preaching and baptizing; but what he did was legal; and when Jesus Christ came to any of John's disciples, He baptized them with fire and the Holy Ghost.[49]

This leads us to a discussion of the twelve "disciples" whom Paul later found at Ephesus, and who claimed to have had the baptism of John. The episode is recorded in Acts 19:1-7:

Paul . . . came to Ephesus: and finding certain disciples,

He said unto them, Have ye received the Holy Ghost since ye believed? And they said unto him, We have not so much as heard whether there be any Holy Ghost.

And he said unto them, Unto what then were ye baptized? And they said, Unto John's baptism.

Then said Paul, John verily baptized with the baptism of repentance, saying unto the people, that they should believe on him which should come after him, that is, on Christ Jesus.

When they heard this, they were baptized in the name of the Lord Jesus.

---

[49]*Teachings*, p. 336.

And when Paul had laid his hands upon them, the Holy Ghost came
on them; and they spake with tongues, and prophesied.
And all the men were about twelve.

This event is often handled by commentators as a case in which
Paul rebaptized some of the disciples of John the Baptist. The explanation is usually given that John's baptism was not really Christian
baptism and therefore was not valid.[50] Such is not the proper explanation since these twelve men were not truly disciples of John the
Baptist at all but only thought they were such. As noted above, the
Prophet Joseph Smith held that John's baptism was legal. In that
case, why would the men at Ephesus need to be baptized again? The
fact is that someone had deceived them at the time of their baptism
and made them think they were receiving John's baptism when
actually they were not. The Prophet Joseph explained the situation
in this manner:

> Again, Luke in his record of the Acts of the Apostles, says: And it
> came to pass, that while Apollos was at Corinth, Paul having passed
> through the upper coasts, came to Ephesus; and finding certain disci-
> ples, he said unto them, Have ye received the Holy Ghost since ye be-
> lieved? And they said unto him, We have not so much as heard
> whether there be any Holy Ghost. And he said unto them, Unto what
> then were ye baptized? And they said: unto John's baptism. Then
> said Paul, John verily baptized with the baptism of repentance, saying
> unto the people, that they should believe on him which should come
> after him, that is on Christ Jesus. When they heard this, they were
> baptized in the name of the Lord Jesus. — And when Paul had laid
> his hands upon them, the Holy Ghost came on them; and they spake
> with tongues, and prophesied.
> From the above witnesses we are informed that baptism was the
> essential point on which they could receive the gift of the Holy Ghost.
> It seems from the reasoning above that some sectarian Jew had been
> baptizing like John, but had forgotten to inform them that there was
> one to follow by the name of Jesus Christ, to baptize with fire and the
> Holy Ghost: — which showed these converts that their first baptism
> was illegal, and when they heard this they were gladly baptized, and
> after hands were laid on them, they received the gifts, according to
> promise, and spake with tongues and prophesied.[51]

---

[50]For example, this is the view taken by Frederic William Farrar, *The Life and
Work of St. Paul* (New York: Cassell and Company, Limited, 1902), p. 362; and
also by W. J. Conybeare and J. S. Howson, *The Life and Epistles of St. Paul*,
(Grand Rapids: William B. Eerdmans Publishing Co., 1964), p. 369. It should be
noted that these commentators discount the validity of John's baptism as being sub-
Christian.

[51]*Teachings*, p. 263.

At another time the Prophet said:

> When Paul came to certain disciples, he asked if they had received the Holy Ghost? They said, No. Who baptized you, then? We were baptized unto John's baptism. No, you were not baptized unto John's baptism, or you would have been baptized by John. And so Paul went and baptized them, for he knew what the true doctrine was, and he knew that John had not baptized them.[52]

There has been a great amount of misunderstanding about this event, and many have supposed that John's baptism was not really valid. The truth is, however, that John was a certified legal administrator for the kingdom of God, but the men at Ephesus had received some other baptism, and not John's.

It should be noted that the question is not whether John the Baptist's authority was valid but whether or not these people at Ephesus had actually been baptized by him. Because John always told his followers about Jesus Christ, who would give them the Holy Ghost, and because these people had not even *heard* of the Holy Ghost, Paul was able to discern that these people had not been baptized by John.

Summary

John the Baptist, then, possessed a spiritual knowledge and understanding of the gospel which indeed was vast. His preaching was vigorous, he successfully executed his appointed mission as a forerunner and proclaimer of the Messiah, and he worthily carried out his assignment to prepare a people and give them the knowledge of salvation.

---

[52]*Teachings*, p. 336.

6
The Record of John

An important item that has not yet been dealt with in this work is the matter of John the Baptist's written account of his ministry and its relationship to the record of John the Beloved. The subject arises particularly in connection with a revelation given to the Prophet Joseph Smith in 1833 (D&C 93).

John's Written Record

In addition to bearing a spoken testimony of the Messiah, it appears that John the Baptist also prepared a written record. This is referred to in Doctrine and Covenants 93:6-18:

> And John saw and bore record of the fulness of my glory, and the fulness of John's record is hereafter to be revealed.
> And he bore record, saying: I saw his glory, that he was in the beginning, before the world was;
> Therefore, in the beginning the Word was, for he was the Word, even the messenger of salvation—
> The light and the Redeemer of the world; the Spirit of truth, who came into the world, because the world was made by him, and in him was the life of men and the light of men.
> The worlds were made by him; men were made by him; all things were made by him, and through him, and of him.
> And I, John, bear record that I beheld his glory, as the glory of the Only Begotten of the Father, full of grace and truth, even the Spirit of truth, which came and dwelt in the flesh, and dwelt among us.

And I, John, saw that he received not of the fulness at the first, but received grace for grace;

And he received not of the fulness at first, but continued from grace to grace, until he received a fulness;

And thus he was called the Son of God, because he received not of the fulness at the first.

And I, John, bear record, and lo, the heavens were opened, and the Holy Ghost descended upon him in the form of a dove, and sat upon him, and there came a voice out of heaven saying: This is my beloved Son.

And I, John, bear record that he received a fulness of the glory of the Father;

And he received all power, both in heaven and on earth, and the glory of the Father was with him, for he dwelt in him.

And it shall come to pass, that if you are faithful you shall receive the fulness of the record of John.

Here we are informed that the "fulness of John's record" is still to come forth, and verse 15 identifies this to be the words of John the Baptist. (Compare John 1:31-34.) We discussed earlier that John, the son of Zebedee, the Beloved Disciple of Jesus, who also wrote the "Gospel of John," had first been a follower of John the Baptist. It appears from the above revelation that he used the Baptist's written record in compiling his own gospel account. Since there are two men involved, each with the name of John, and the quotation from the Doctrine and Covenants has the flavor of the Gospel of John, the matter is a little confusing. However, that the passage in the Doctrine and Covenants has particular reference to the record of John the Baptist was the view held by both Pres. John Taylor and Elder Orson Pratt. In the heading to chapter six of his book *The Mediation and Atonement*, President Taylor makes reference to the "Record of John the Baptist." The subsequent discussion in that chapter uses the material from Doctrine and Covenants 93:6-18. A similar notation relating to the "Record of John the Baptist" is likewise found in the table of contents for chapter six of *The Mediation and Atonement*.[53]

The matter of a written record by John the Baptist was discussed by Elder Orson Pratt in a discourse in the Ogden Tabernacle on Sunday, May 18, 1873, in which he said:

Not only the records of the ancient inhabitants of this land are to come forth, but the records of those who slept on the eastern hemi-

[53]John Taylor, *An Examination into and an Elucidation of the Great Principle of the Mediation and Atonement of Our Lord and Savior Jesus Christ* (Salt Lake City: Stevens and Wallis, Inc., 1950), table of contents and pp. 55, 59. I have checked the original edition and all subsequent printings of the book, and they all contain these references to the record of John the Baptist.

sphere. The records of John, him who baptized the Lamb of God, are yet to be revealed. We are informed in the book of Doctrine and Covenants, page 245 [section 93:18 in current editions], that the fullness of the record of John, is to be revealed to the Latter-day Saints.[54]

Elder Bruce R. McConkie also affirms that John the Baptist kept a written record:

> From latter-day revelation we learn that the material in the forepart of the gospel of John (the Apostle, Revelator, and Beloved Disciple) was written originally by John the Baptist. By revelation the Lord restored to Joseph Smith part of what John the Baptist had written and promised to reveal the balance when men became sufficiently faithful to warrant receiving it. (D&C 93:6-18.) . . .
>
> Even without revelation, however, it should be evident that John the Baptist had something to do with the recording of events in the forepart of John's gospel, for some of the occurrences include his conversations with the Jews and a record of what he saw when our Lord was baptized — all of which matters would have been unknown to John the Apostle whose ministry began somewhat later than that of the Baptist's. There is little doubt but that the Beloved Disciple had before him the Baptist's account when he wrote his gospel. The latter John either copied or paraphrased what the earlier prophet of the same name had written.[55]

John the Baptist and John the Beloved

There seems to be a greater affinity between the Baptist and the Beloved Disciple John than is found between the Baptist and either Matthew, Mark, or Luke. It is from the Gospel of John that we learn the deepest and most intimate things about John the Baptist. Matthew, Mark, and Luke tell us that John is great, but it is from the Gospel of John that we learn *why* he is great. The Baptist's greatest witness comes to us through John's Gospel, which deals with the Baptist's testimony after he had seen the Holy Ghost descend upon Jesus. And it is through John's Gospel also that we have the Baptist's testimony to his own disciples. This should not be too surprising, since John the Beloved had been a disciple of John the Baptist and consequently would have had opportunity to be well acquainted with both the man and his written record. Thus it appears that John the Beloved made use of John the Baptist's record in preparing the Gospel of John.

---

[54]Orson Pratt in *Journal of Discourses*, 26 vols. (London: Latter-day Saints' Book Depot, 1855-86), 16:58.

[55]*Doctrinal New Testament Commentary*, 1:70-71.

81

This raises the point that perhaps some of the testimonies about Christ which appear in the Gospel of John, and which traditionally have been thought of as being the exclusive writing of the Beloved Disciple, may in reality be a testimony of Christ given first by John the Baptist. There are at least three notable and important possibilities of this found in the Gospel of John. The first is the material contained in John 1:1-27, which serves as a prologue to identify the roles of both Jesus and John the Baptist. Although in its present form, arrangement, and location this material is probably the work of John the Beloved, it is possible that much of the information represents a transcript originally taken from the record of John the Baptist. Thus John the Baptist's written record might well identify Jesus as the Creator and make references to his premortal existence. This conclusion is strengthened if one accepts Doctrine and Covenants 93:6-18 as having some connection with a record of John the Baptist. The similarity of ideas is striking. The form in which we have received it is from John the Beloved, but it may well represent the testimony of John the Baptist. And, of course, there is nothing wrong with two men having the same testimony about the Son of God.

The second instance is found in John 1:19-36, which seems to have many possibilities of being rooted in the written record of John the Baptist. This group of verses even begins with the statement, "And this is the record [i.e., testimony, witness, etc.] of John" (verse 19) and consists of John the Baptist's testimony of himself and of Christ. Of particular note is the Baptist's account of seeing the Holy Ghost descend upon Jesus as a special sign by which John might identify Jesus as the Messiah. (Compare John 1:31-34 with D&C 93:15.)

The third instance is found in John 3:27-36 and contains the Baptist's testimony to his own disciples concerning Christ's divinity. Many commentators feel that only verses 27 through 30 are the words of the Baptist, and forthwith designate verses 31 through 36 as a commentary or reflection by John the Beloved.[56] However, neither the context nor the content of the passage suggests any reasons why these words could not have been spoken by the Baptist, and with our wider understanding of John the Baptist's great knowledge of the gospel and his own written account, there is strong reason for considering these later verses (31 through 36) the continued testimony of John the Baptist.[57]

---

[56]See, for example, Giuseppe Ricciotti, *The Life of Christ* (Milwaukee: The Bruce Publishing Company, 1947), pp. 291-92, 294; Buttrick, et al., *The Interpreter's Bible*, 8:517; William Barclay, *The Gospel of John*, 2 vols. (Philadelphia: The Westminster Press, 1956), 1:136.

[57]The reader will find the entire passage (verses 27 through 36) identified as the Baptist's testimony in Clark, *Our Lord of the Gospels*, pp. 195-96; in McConkie,

There can be little question of John the Baptist's ability to write, for, as we have been shown by the Dead Sea Scrolls, that period of time was a very literacy-oriented age among the Jews, even among the desert dwellers. Reading and writing apparently were commonly practiced. Sacred history shows that the prophets of God have always been commanded to keep records, from Adam to the present time, so why not John? When the Baptist did the actual writing we are not informed. Perhaps the long months in prison afforded him this opportunity, if he had not accomplished it sooner.

We can eagerly await the time when the fulness of John's record will be revealed and will be available for study, for doubtless we will learn much from it about the mission of John the Baptist and the ministry of the Savior, and something concerning textual criticism of the Gospel of John and perhaps of the books of Matthew, Mark, and Luke also.

Doctrinal New Testament Commentary, 1:145-48; in Talmage, *Jesus the Christ,* p. 164; and in a work by a French scholar of the late nineteenth century, Frederic Godet, *Commentary on the Gospel of John,* 2 vols. (New York: Funk and Wagnalls, Publishers, 1886), 1:410-15, 539-41. Godet presents a detailed argument favoring John the Baptist's authorship of these verses and defends his point in terms of content, vocabulary, verb tense, context, and what he calls the "spirit of the text." He states: "All the details of the discourse are in harmony with the character of the person of the Baptist. There is not a word which cannot be fully explained in his mouth" (p. 414).

7

Arrest, Imprisonment, and Death

The Closing Scenes of John's Public Ministry

In the summer months following the baptism of Jesus, John was baptizing at Aenon, near Salim, "because there was much water there" (John 3:23). Many people came and were baptized. Consistent with the dating system adopted for this study, John's activities at Aenon would probably have been in the summer and autumn of A.D. 27. It was apparently also at Aenon that John gave his last recorded testimony of Christ and urged his disciples to follow Jesus in preference to himself. But even though John always faithfully bore witness that Jesus is the Messiah and testified that he himself was much inferior to Jesus, some of John's disciples showed a reluctance to leave him.

It is not known with certainty today just where "Aenon near to Salim" was. The record states that "there was much water there," but beyond this we have little to identify it. *Aenon* is a Greek word meaning "springs," and historians speak of several ancient Salims, any of which might qualify as the particular area of the closing scenes of John's public ministry. Some commentators favor Samaria as the probable location.[58] If this is the correct identification, it suggests a Samarian ministry for John, which possibly contributed to Jesus' sub-

---

[58]Scobie, *John the Baptist*, pp. 163-65; see also Farrar, *The Life of Christ* (Portland: Fountain Publications, 1960), p. 170, footnote.

sequent success in Samaria, as it would seem natural for Jesus to travel and preach over the same ground where his forerunner had prepared the way.

Other scholars place Aenon in Scythopolis in Decapolis,[59] or even in Judea.[60] While it probably does not matter much to us today where the ancient site was, it may have meant something very particular to John, since he may have gone there not only because of its much water but because he needed a place to go outside of the domain of Herod. Subsequent events show that John had incurred the envy of the Pharisees and also of Herod, and it is reasonable to conclude that he sought a place of refuge where he would be out of Herod's reach and yet where he could continue his preaching and baptizing. Since Herod's political domain at this time consisted of Galilee and Perea, John would be relatively safe in the wilderness areas of either Judea, Decapolis, or Samaria.

Nothing is recorded from May to December regarding either John or Jesus beyond the mention that Jesus was baptizing in Judea with his disciples and that John was baptizing at Aenon near Salim, for he had not yet been cast into prison (John 3:22-24). It was, however, a time of turmoil and trouble for both John and Jesus, and the hatred of the Jewish rulers was particularly great. This is recorded in the fourth chapter of the Gospel of John. Note that the Inspired Version gives greater emphasis to the envy of the Jews:

King James Version	Inspired Version
1 When therefore the Lord knew how the Pharisees had heard that Jesus made and baptized more disciples than John,	1 When therefore the *Pharisees had heard* that Jesus made and baptized more disciples than John,
	2 They sought more diligently some means that they might put him to death; for many received John as a prophet, but they believed not on Jesus.
2 (Though Jesus himself baptized not, but his disciples,)	3 *Now the Lord knew this,* though *he* himself baptized not *so many as* his disciples;
	4 For he suffered them for an example, preferring one another.

[59]James Hastings, ed., *Dictionary of the Bible* (New York: Charles Scribner's Sons, 1963), pp. 101, 878. Also Ricciotti, *The Life of Christ,* p. 270. See also the counterarguments presented in the references given in footnote 58, above.

[60]Gale, *John the Baptist,* pp. 130-32. While Gale does not personally subscribe to the Judean location for Aenon, he discusses the reasoning given by those who do.

| 3 He left Judaea, and departed again into Galilee. | 5 *And* he left Judea, and departed again into Galilee. |

The reason Jesus left Judea to go into Galilee was probably to avoid the extreme hatred of the Pharisees in Judea, who at this time "sought more diligently some means that they might put him to death."

This proved to be John's last summer of freedom. He had begun his preaching and baptizing about a year or so earlier (summer, A.D. 26) in Judea near the region of the Jordan River, and had baptized Jesus after perhaps about six to nine months of his ministry. It appears that sometime during the late summer or autumn of A.D. 27 he fell into disfavor with the Judean ruling family. He particularly offended Herodias, the wife of Herod, by his insistence that it was not right for Herod to have her, since she was legally the wife of Herod's half-brother, Philip. This angered Herodias to the point that she would have killed John if she could, but because John was a prophet Herod looked upon him with awe and for a time protected him (Mark 6:17-20). According to Josephus, however, Herod himself had some misgivings about John's great popularity with the people, and so imprisoned him.[61]

This marital situation of Herod's, to which John objected, was somewhat complex. Herod was originally married to the daughter of Aretas, the king of Arabia, but on a visit to Rome he stayed with his half-brother Philip and fell in love with Philip's wife, Herodias. This was an opportunity for Herodias. Her husband, Philip, had no title and ruled no province. In her estimation he was a "nobody" and, while married to him, she was simply a housewife. As Herod's wife she would be a queen. So she agreed to marry Herod on condition that he divorce his first wife. With her daughter Salome, she left Philip and their residence in Rome and became the wife of Herod the King, ruler of Galilee and Perea.

To further complicate the relationship, Herodias was not only Herod's sister-in-law, but also his niece, being the daughter of Aristobulus, Herod's half-brother. She was married, therefore, first to one uncle and now to another uncle.

Meanwhile, as this situation was developing, Herod's first wife became aware of what was going on and fled to her father, King Aretas, in Arabia, whereupon, for this and other reasons, Aretas in due time raised an army and made war upon Herod and in A.D. 36 defeated him.[62]

---

[61]*Antiquities*, XVIII:5:2.

[62]*Antiquities*, XVIII:5:1-2. This is Aretas IV, who was king of Arabia from 9 B.C. to A.D. 40, and is the same Aretas mentioned by Paul in 2 Corinthians 11:32.

John's Arrest

Of the arrest of John the scriptures simply state that "Herod had laid hold on John, and bound him, and put him in prison" (Matthew 14:3; also Mark 6:17; Luke 3:19-20).

Matthew says that Jesus was in Judea at this time, and, knowing "that John was cast into prison, he departed into Galilee (Matthew 4:12). This is probably the same departure into Galilee mentioned in John 4:1-3, quoted above.

There are some interesting circumstances associated with both the reasons for and the mechanics of John's arrest. Somewhat conflicting reports are given as to the cause of John's imprisonment. According to Mark, John was imprisoned because he had infuriated Herod and Herodias by questioning the validity of their marriage (Mark 6:17-19). However, Josephus says that John was imprisoned because he was becoming so popular and commanded such a following that Herod feared his political power. Although Josephus confirms the matter of Herod's unlawful marriage, he does not associate it as a factor in John's imprisonment.[63]

Whatever the reasons, the sources do agree that John was imprisoned at the command of Herod. It may be that both causes were contributory: the political factor may have been the initial cause of his imprisonment, so far as Herod was personally concerned, and pretending to be primarily concerned about the domestic issue may have been Herod's way of placating the uneasy Herodias.

The Pharisees may have collaborated with Herod in the capture and arrest of John. Although the scriptural record does not categorically confirm this, there seems to be enough circumstantial evidence to warrant such a conclusion. First, the Pharisees were antagonistic to John (Luke 7:20-30) and openly denied the legitimacy of his baptism. Secondly, the King James Version says that John was "cast" into prison (Matthew 4:12), but the meaning of the Greek word in this instance is more than "cast": it carries the sense of being "delivered up." This is substantiated by the marginal reading in the King James Version,[64] and appears in the texts of the American Standard Verson,[65] the Confraternity (Catholic) Bible,[66] and the Syrian manuscripts translated by Lamsa.[67] Each of these contains the

---

It is a dynastic title, not a personal name. (See Hastings, *Dictionary of the Bible*, p. 52.)

[63] *Antiquities*, XVIII:5:1-2.
[64] "Or, *delivered up.*"
[65] ". . . was delivered up . . ."
[66] ". . . had been delivered up . . ."
[67] "John was delivered and imprisoned."

thought that John was "delivered up" into prison. Thirdly, when John was "delivered up and imprisoned" Jesus immediately left the area, apparently for the safety of himself and his disciples.

That it is really the Pharisees, and not Herod only, who are the "enemy" is seen by the fact that Jesus went into Galilee, which was still under Herod's jurisdiction. If Herod had been the real enemy, Jesus would still have been in danger in Galilee. But while Galilee was still Herod's domain, it was somewhat out of reach of the Judean Pharisees who were repeatedly laying snares to catch John and/or Jesus. Possibly John had become a victim of the devices of the Pharisees and somehow had been lured by them into Herod's area and delivered into Herod's custody; then perhaps Jesus, knowing what had happened, left Judea and went into Galilee where the situation was less tense. This idea is strengthened by the Lord's observation to Peter, James, and John that the Jews "have done unto him [John] whatsoever they listed" and that "likewise shall also the Son of man suffer of them" (Matthew 17:12-13). Since it is known that the Pharisees were active in the arrest and crucifixion of Jesus, it follows from the Savior's statement that they "likewise" were agents in the arrest and imprisonment of John.

This assumption is further supported by a subsequent encounter in Galilee between Jesus and a delegation of the Pharisees. In this instance the Pharisees — who are never identified as friends of Jesus — came to him in Galilee and said, "Get thee out, and depart hence: for Herod will kill thee" (Luke 13:31). Although it is remotely possible that these particular Pharisees were honestly concerned for the welfare of Jesus and that this warning to him was prompted by a genuine interest for his bodily safety, it seems more likely that the Pharisees were only feigning friendship for Jesus, and that their real motive was to lure Jesus out of Galilee and back into Judea, where Herod had no jurisdiction but where Jesus would fall into the hands of the Jewish rulers. The Lord's reply to them is instructive. The Pharisees and Herod had little in common, except a dislike for Jesus; yet Jesus' reply indicates that he knew that the Pharisees and Herod were in communication with one another. Said he, "Go ye, and tell that fox . . . I must walk to day, and to morrow, and the day following: for it cannot be that a prophet perish out of Jerusalem" (Luke 13:32-33). Such a reply not only gave notice to the Pharisees that Jesus was not about to buy their supposed act of friendship, but also a message to them — and to Herod — that Jesus' death, when it did occur, would not be in Galilee but in Jerusalem, and he did not fear what they could do to him in Galilee. It is likely that these clever Pharisees, who had successfully plotted with Herod in the capture of

John, were now attempting the same kind of strategy (in reverse) to capture Jesus.

Another passage that further attests to the collusion between the Pharisees and Herod is found in Mark 3:6, which states that the Pharisees plotted with the Herodians to destroy Jesus. Hate makes strange bedfellows. The Jewish rulers had no love for the Herodians. The Pharisees hated Herod and all who supported him; but they hated Jesus even more, and were willing to unite with their national enemies, the Herodians, to destroy him.

The wisdom of God is always greater than the craftiness of men or the cunning of the devil, and had heaven so desired, the machinations of evil men could never silence a prophet of God. But sometimes the righteous are permitted to be slain after they have completed their missions, that they might be honored and the wicked condemned. (Compare Alma 14:11-13; D&C 136:39.)

John's Imprisonment

The scriptural record does not say where the prison was located, but Josephus asserts that it was in Herod's castle at Machaerus near the eastern border of the Dead Sea.[68] This would be some fifty miles east and a little south of Jerusalem.

How long John was imprisoned is not stated, but he was placed in prison sometime near the end of the first year of Jesus' ministry, and probably remained in prison for at least a year, maybe a little longer.

It appears that John was not in solitary confinement, for his disciples had some freedom to come and go, but it must have been extremely difficult for this active man of the desert to be restricted to a dungeon cell. The scripture says that Herod "laid hold on John, and bound him" (Matthew 14:3), which most certainly means he was in chains.[69] Also, some interpret the words "they have done unto

---

[68]*Antiquities*, XVIII:5:1-2. Also, J. A. Thompson gives this account of Machaerus: "At the extreme south of the area, on the edge of the Nabataean kingdom, was the fortress of Machaerus, situated on an isolated hill and surrounded by a wall. It was first built by Alexander Jannaeus [about 100 B.C.], but was razed by the Romans in 63 B.C. Herod the Great rebuilt it between 25 and 13 B.C. Later it came into the territory of Antipas, and here, according to Josephus, John the Baptist met his death. The town is not mentioned in the New Testament. Today there is a considerable area of ruins awaiting serious excavation" (*The Bible and Archaeology*, p. 360).

[69]This is the reading of the New English Bible and the New American Bible (Catholic), which use "chains" in preference to the King James's "bonds." See Mark 6:17.

him [John] whatsoever they listed" to mean that John was tortured, since torture was a common treatment of prisoners in that day.[70]

The Inspired Version adds a matter of great interest relative to John's imprisonment, and in so doing likewise attests to Jesus' great compassion and high regard for John. The passage is Matthew 4:11: "Jesus knew that John was cast into prison, and he sent angels, and ... they came and ministered unto him."[71] In no other text or source do we find information suggesting that John was visited by angels during his imprisonment, but this thought has a warm and comforting aspect to it.

John Sends Messengers to Jesus

During the months while John was a prisoner, Jesus' fame continually increased. It was said of Jesus that "a great prophet is risen up among us," and this word concerning him "went forth throughout all Judaea, and throughout all the region round about" (Luke 7:16-17). The disciples of John, knowing of this great reputation of Jesus, came to the Baptist in prison and "shewed him of all these things" (Luke 7:18). The subsequent events are recorded in Luke 7:19-23:

> And John calling unto him two of his disciples sent them to Jesus, saying, Art thou he that should come? or look we for another?
>
> When the men were come unto him, they said, John the Baptist hath sent us unto thee, saying, Art thou he that should come? or look we for another?
>
> And in that same hour he cured many of their infirmities and plagues, and of evil spirits; and unto many that were blind he gave sight.
>
> Then Jesus answering said unto them, Go your way, and tell John what things ye have seen and heard; how that the blind see, the lame walk, the lepers are cleansed, the deaf hear, the dead are raised, to the poor the gospel is preached.
>
> And blessed is he, whosoever shall not be offended in me.[72]

---

[70]This is the view of Cunningham Geikie, *The Life and Words of Christ*, 2 vols. (New York: D. Appleton and Company, 1879), 1:420.

[71]The exact text of the original manuscript of the Inspired Version is even more specific and reads: "And now Jesus new [sic] that John was cast into prison and he sent angels and behold they came and ministered unto him (John)" (New Testament Manuscript No. 1, p. 7, ll. 14-16 [Courtesy of The Reorganized Church of Jesus Christ of Latter Day Saints, Independence, Missouri, who permitted me to examine the manuscript]).

[72]The Inspired Version reads the same for Luke, but has the following variant reading in the corresponding material from Matthew 11:6: "And blessed is *John*, and whosoever shall not be offended in me."

The question often arises why John would send his disciples to ask such a question of Jesus. Many have wondered if it was possible that John himself was not sure of Christ's identity and divine calling. However, we must remember that John's last recorded testimony was to his disciples when they were concerned about the growing popularity of Jesus. John reminded them that he himself was not the Messiah, and that they should leave him and follow Jesus. That was several months prior to the present event under discussion. It appears that one of the difficulties experienced by John was successfully persuading his disciples to forsake him and become the disciples of Jesus Christ, of whom he had borne witness. Now, months after the baptism of Jesus and after John's repeated efforts to persuade them, John found some of his disciples still reluctant to detach themselves from him and to follow their true Master. It seems most consistent to identify John's motive in sending the two disciples to Jesus as one of persuasion for them, rather than of reassurance for himself. The question they were to put to Jesus was for their edification, not for his own. John knew, as no one else knew, who Jesus was, and he had known it for a long time. He had had revelation from heaven to this effect: he had seen with his eyes, he had heard with his ears, and he had the testimony of the Holy Ghost. He even had received the ministry of angels while in the prison. The most satisfactory answer seems to be that John sent his disciples to question Jesus about his identity so that they themselves would at long last realize the truth of what John had been testifying for these many months. This approach seems consistent with John's sure knowledge of the Redeemer, his known testimony to his disciples, and the natural reluctance of his disciples to leave him.

Perhaps a point should be made here that there was not an antagonism between Jesus and John. A man did not have to utterly forsake and reject John in order to accept Jesus. But Jesus was the Son of God, and John was his prophet. There is no equal comparison between the two, and John did not want any mistaken notions among his own associates about the relative stations of himself and his Master.

After the two messengers had left Jesus to return to John in prison, Jesus began to speak to the multitude concerning John and said, among other things, that "among them that are born of women there hath not risen a greater than John the Baptist" (Matthew 11:11; also Luke 7:24-28).

What effect this experience had on the two disciples we are not told. We know nothing of their impressions from personally meeting the Master or of their conversation with one another while returning to

John in the dungeon. And there would have been plenty of opportunity to discuss the matter, since they had contacted Jesus in Galilee and were now returning to John at Machaerus near the eastern shore of the Dead Sea, a distance of not less than one hundred miles. Whatever their mode of travel, such a trip would consume two or three days. It would be interesting to know of their reunion with John and of the exchange of words as they told him what they had seen and heard from Jesus. But none of these things, if recorded, are currently available to us.

Death of a Prophet

As was discussed in chapter four, sometime during John's ministry he had a personal and firsthand relationship with Herod. It is not clear from the scriptures when this was, but it is probable that they met face to face while John was a free man, and that John counseled the king. This relationship may also have continued even while John was a prisoner in the king's castle at Machaerus. The precise times and circumstances are not known to us, but the scriptures certify that Herod had a certain high regard and awe for John and at times was willing to obey his counsel. This is especially important to us in a discussion of John's martyrdom.

Mark 6:14-29 presents the following account of the events that led to the death of John:

> And king Herod heard of him; (for his name was spread abroad:) and he said, That John the Baptist was risen from the dead, and therefore mighty works do shew forth themselves in him.
> Others said, That it is Elias. And others said, That it is a prophet, or as one of the prophets.
> But when Herod heard thereof, he said, It is John, whom I beheaded: he is risen from the dead.
> For Herod himself had sent forth and laid hold upon John, and bound him in prison for Herodias' sake, his brother Philip's wife: for he had married her.
> For John had said unto Herod, It is not lawful for thee to have thy brother's wife.
> Therefore Herodias had a quarrel against him, and would have killed him; but she could not:

Verse 21 in the Inspired Version clarifies the corresponding passage in the King James Version:

King James Version	Inspired Version
20 For Herod feared John, knowing that he was a just man	21 For Herod feared John, knowing that he was a just man,

93

and an holy, and observed him; and when he heard him, he did many things, and heard him gladly.

and a holy *man*, and one who feared God and observed *to worship* him; and when he heard him he did many things *for him*, and heard him gladly.

The King James Version continues:

Mark 6:21 And when a convenient day was come, that Herod on his birthday made a supper to his lords, high captains, and chief estates of Galilee;

6:22 And when the daughter of the said Herodias came in, and danced, and pleased Herod and them that sat with him, the king said unto the damsel, Ask of me whatsoever thou wilt, and I will give it thee.

6:23 And he sware unto her, Whatsoever thou shalt ask of me, I will give it thee, unto the half of my kingdom.

6:24 And she went forth, and said unto her mother, What shall I ask? And she said, The head of John the Baptist.

6:25 And she came in straightway with haste unto the king, and asked, saying, I will that thou give me by and by in a charger the head of John the Baptist.

6:26 And the king was exceeding sorry; yet for his oath's sake, and for their sakes which sat with him, he would not reject her.

6:27 And immediately the king sent an executioner, and commanded his head to be brought: and he went and beheaded him in the prison,

6:28 And brought his head in a charger, and gave it to the damsel: and the damsel gave it to her mother.

6:29 And when his disciples heard of it, they came and took up his corpse, and laid it in a tomb.

This passage, especially as presented in the Inspired Version, indicates that Herod regarded John as a "holy man . . . and heard him gladly," and "did many things for him." What the many things were that Herod did for John are not specified, but they appear to have included temporarily protecting John from Herodias, who, according to the record, "would have killed him," but could not, because of Herod's fear of John (verses 19-20). Perhaps Herod also protected John for a time from the Pharisees and Jewish rulers.

That Herod did protect John is borne out by several variant translations, especially of the verb translated in the King James Version as "observed." Mark says that "Herod feared John . . . and observed him" (verse 20). The marginal reading of the King James Version causes the verse to read, "For Herod feared John . . . and kept him safe." The Catholic Confraternity Bible reads, "For Herod feared John . . . and protected him." This is confirmed by Luther's German translation, which uses the word *verwahrte*, meaning that Herod

94

"preserved" or "protected" John. This makes a much stronger declaration than simply to say that Herod "observed" John.[73]

At any rate, there were those in Herod's household who were believers. In Matthew 14:1-2 and Luke 9:7, 9 we read that when Herod heard of the fame of Jesus — and supposing him to be John the Baptist risen from the dead — he inquired of his servants concerning it. Why would Herod inquire of his servants? What were they supposed to know about Jesus or John? Luke (8:3) tells us that one of the followers of Jesus was "Joanna the wife of Chuza Herod's steward." Later, in Acts 13:1, we learn that "there were in the church . . . certain prophets and teachers," among whom was Manaen, who "had been brought up with Herod the tetrarch." Herod must have known of these people in his own household; therefore, desperate, haunted by the thought that John was risen from the dead, he inquired among those who were close to him and who he thought could give him the information he desired.

We cannot help but wonder if John laid the groundwork for the faith of these two persons of Herod's household. Herod and John must have had several face-to-face contacts, and Herod's servants may have been present on some of these occasions and heard John's testimony. Years later Paul affirmed that while he was a prisoner in Rome he gave his message to some of Caesar's palace (Philippians 1:12-13), and it is possible that John the Baptist was able to do the same in Herod's palace.

The respect and awe that Herod had for John, however, were soon overruled by other desires. To save face before those who were at the supper, to keep his oath, and maybe even to enjoy a possible new "adventure" with the dancing girl, Herod was maneuvered by his wife into issuing the death sentence for John the Baptist. Whatever kind of a dance it was that the girl performed (who is not named in scripture, but is identified as *Salome*[74]), it was so well done that it caused the king to recklessly promise her anything she wished, even to "half of his kingdom." Matthew notes that she danced "in the midst" of the crowd (Matthew 14:6, marginal reading). Steinmann thinks that the girl probably danced in the nude,[75] but Geikie seems to think otherwise on the basis that such was not the custom of the day.[76] Salome, however, was brought up in pagan Rome, and the

---

[73]The word "observed" as used in the King James Version includes the idea of respect or reverence. Such usage is obsolete today, but was common in A.D. 1611.

[74]Hastings, *Dictionary of the Bible*, p. 878.

[75]Jean Steinmann, *Saint John the Baptist and the Desert Tradition*, trans. Michael Boyes (New York: Harper and Brothers [1958]), p. 103.

[76]*The Life and Words of Christ*, 1:430.

game she and her mother were playing was "for keeps." Herodias masterminded the whole affair, and it is not likely she would overlook any opportunity she thought would be impressive, regardless of the custom of the time.

The record states that the king was "exceeding sorry" to issue an order for the death of John. The sorrow was probably genuine, for he feared that John was a prophet and he knew that John was very popular among the people. That Herod could not forget the deed is reflected in his later mistaking Jesus for John and thinking that John had risen from the dead. His conscience must have bothered and even haunted him to think that John had returned from the dead and that "mighty works" were now manifest in him. John had done no miracles in his ministry (John 10:41), but as a man raised from the dead (as Herod supposed), he would quite possibly have had miraculous powers. This is probably why the emphasis is given to Herod's statement that "therefore mighty works do shew forth themselves in him" (Matthew 14:2). Herod's apprehension in this instance is an illustration of the principle that the "wicked flee when no man pursueth: but the righteous are bold as a lion" (Proverbs 28:1).

Meanwhile, the heinousness of the crime weighed upon the minds of many besides Herod. Josephus writes that when Herod's army was defeated by King Aretas, many people attributed the defeat to the curse of God upon Herod for killing John.[77]

It is interesting that Herod, the king, should be outmaneuvered by his wife and by a dancing girl. His appetite and lust for the girl's bodily charms snared him into a compromising situation for which he afterward was very sorry. The whole caper was brought about in the first place because of his libidinous desire for Herodias, whom he had spirited away from Philip, and whom it was not lawful for him to have. It was bodily lust and passion that had caused him to forsake his wife, the daughter of Aretas, for Herodias, and now it was more of the same that made him vulnerable to the scheming of Herodias in her plan to make him destroy the very man he had previously protected. Herodias, above all others, knew what kind of a man Herod was. She knew his weakness for the flesh.

Since Herodias wished to kill John but could not because Herod *protected* him, she set about to devise a method not only to get John killed, but to get Herod to do it. Herod had shown himself to be a man of much passion, with fleeting moments of good intention, but with little self-control and even less manly discipline. Herodias herself had beguiled him in their days at Rome, and now she again

---

[77]*Antiquities*, XVIII:5:1.

played upon his weaknesses. But this time she would use a younger woman: Salome would be the bait. Jesus was later to refer to Herod as "that fox" (Luke 13:32). Since Herod was cunning but not strong, this was an apt description. His character was much more reminiscent of a fox than a lion.

The story of Herodias's plans for the destruction of John continues in the King James Version, "And when a convenient day was come, that Herod on his birthday made a supper to his lords . . ." (Mark 6:21). The situation is more emphatically expressed by the New English Bible in this manner: *"Herodias found her opportunity* when Herod on his birthday gave a banquet to his chief officials." Thus the New English Bible more fully picks up the intended flavor of the passage than does the King James Version, by emphasizing that when Herodias was frustrated in her initial desire to kill John because Herod protected him, she sought for and found an "opportunity" to manipulate Herod into compliance with her wishes. Herodias's unladylike behavior in this event more than justifies all that John the Baptist had said about her.

In Herod, Herodias, and John, we see a trio similar to an earlier one in Israel's history: King Ahab, his wife, Jezebel, and the prophet Elijah. In that earlier day, Jezebel schemed and outclassed her morally weak husband-king and caused the death of some of the Lord's prophets. In Jezebel's day as in Herodias's, the man of God rebuked their wickedness and in turn incurred their burning hatred. What was the final outcome for Herod? As noted before, Herod's army was defeated by the army of Aretas; later Herod fell out of favor with the Emperor Caligula and in A.D. 39 was deposed and banished to Gaul.

In one sense, John was the first Christian martyr of the meridian of time, although it is Stephen (Acts 7:59) who is generally so designated.

Burial

The time was probably the winter of A.D. 28-29; the son of Elisabeth and Zacharias, now in his thirty-third year, was dead at the hands of Herod Antipas. More than thirty years earlier, Antipas's father, Herod the Great, had caused the death of Zacharias, the father of John.

John's disciples obtained his body, which they buried in a tomb, and then sought out Jesus in Galilee and told him what had happened (Mark 6:29-30). It is noteworthy that at this dreary hour in their lives John's disciples went to Jesus. This would be exactly what John would want them to do. Perhaps the shock of John's violent death had accomplished what John himself had not been able to do: to persuade them to prefer Jesus to himself. John's witness and testimony was now an even greater reality to them than it had been while he lived. When they came to Jesus he would comfort them and draw them closer to himself.

From Mark's account we learn that the Twelve were on missions at the time of John's death, but returned soon thereafter (Mark 6:7, 12, 30). Matthew tells us that when Jesus in Galilee heard that John was beheaded, he departed "by ship into a desert place apart" with his disciples (Matthew 14:13). Many followed them, and it was at this time that Jesus miraculously fed the five thousand (Matthew 14:13-18). It is perhaps significant also that by going out of Galilee and into the desert east of the sea of Galilee — which is the only way they could go by ship — Jesus left Herod Antipas's domain and entered the tetrarchy of Herod Philip. This may have been a safety measure.

Resurrection of John

Thus had ended the mortal ministry of one of God's noblest men. His earthly mission was completed; he had kept himself unspotted from the world and had testified against the evils of his day. He made straight the highway of his God, announced the presence of the Messiah, baptized the very Son of God, laid the groundwork for the overthrow of the kingdom of the Jews, and prepared a people. Last of all, he suffered a martyr's violent death. Soon, in perhaps about a year and a half, the Messiah himself would be slain and his body placed in a tomb. But the Messiah had power over the grave. He would break the bands of death and come forth with his resurrected glorified body, no more to be maimed or bruised. And the resurrection of the Messiah would bring to pass the resurrection of all men, including John the Baptist.

As recorded in a divine communication to Joseph Smith, John came forth from the tomb at a time immediately following Jesus' own resurrection (D&C 133:55) and is referred to as being "with Christ in his resurrection."

8
John
and Jesus

The scriptures portray a vivid relationship between John the Baptist and Jesus. John loved his Master and the Master loved John. As noted earlier, their mothers, Elisabeth and Mary, were cousins and discussed with one another the future missions of their yet unborn sons. Each mother knew of the special and holy missions of both children. Mary's firstborn was to be named Jesus and was the very Son of God, the Messiah and Savior of the world. Elisabeth's son, born when she was old, was to be named John and was the herald and forerunner to prepare the way before the Messiah. John was born about six months before Jesus.

There is no direct evidence that John and Jesus ever met or knew each other as boys,[78] but certainly each of the mothers must have told her own son about the other.

John's Testimony of Jesus Christ

When John was about thirty years of age he came into the region of the Jordan River preaching the gospel, baptizing, and declaring that the Messiah was soon to appear. John fulfilled his divine commission not only by teaching the principles of the gospel and proclaiming that the Messiah was about to make an appearance, but, most of all— *after* he had baptized Jesus in water and beheld the Holy Ghost

---

[78]See the discussion on this item in chapter three.

descend upon him — by openly identifying Jesus as the Messiah and Son of God.

John stirred up the people and aroused the nation. He preached repentance and baptized the believers for the remission of sins, to prepare them for the coming of the Lord, and he gave positive identification of the Messiah by pointing Jesus out in person to the multitudes and declaring him to be the long-awaited Son of God.

John used simple eloquence in describing his own relationship to Jesus. So effective and successful was John as a preacher that many supposed that he was the Messiah of whom the prophets had spoken. But John never forgot his place and true position. To the multitudes he explained that he himself was the forerunner and was not able to bear the shoes of the Messiah; indeed, he said he was not even worthy to unloose the latchet of the Messiah's footwear. He pointed out that he himself baptized with water, but that the Messiah would baptize not only with water but with fire and the Holy Ghost (Mark 1:6, I.V.; John 1:28, I.V.).

To the delegation sent to him from the Pharisees John openly avowed that he was not the Christ but was the voice of one crying in the wilderness to make a path straight for the Christ. He did not deny that he was Elias, but insisted, "I am not the Christ" (John 1:21-22, I.V.).

To his own disciples as well, John carefully explained that he himself was not the Christ. "Jesus," he said in effect, "is the bridegroom; I am the friend of the bridegroom, whose joy is in making ready for him." (See John 3:28-30.) Speaking further to his disciples of the contrast between his own position and that of the Messiah, John demonstrated his singleness of purpose:

> He must increase, but I must decrease. He that cometh from above is above all: he that is of the earth [i.e., John himself] is earthly. [John 3:30-31.]

John's threefold testimony was (1) that the Messiah would come, (2) that the Messiah had come and Jesus was that Messiah, and (3) that John's disciples should leave him and follow Jesus. John was true to his trust and never went beyond his bounds and privileges. His witness of Christ was clear and effective.

Although he did not perform any miracles, John effectively fulfilled his mission to prepare a people for the Lord; and when Jesus came among them both preaching and performing miracles in the power of his godliness, the people exclaimed, "John did no miracle: but all things that John spake of this man were true" (John 10:41). This is a forthright attestation to the effectiveness of John's ministry.

100

Jesus' Testimony of John

The relationship between John and Jesus was mutually enjoyed. Not only did John bear witness of Jesus, but Jesus likewise defended John's mission and publicly praised him. Speaking to the Pharisees who had sent a delegation to inquire of John, Jesus said, "Ye sent unto John, and he bare witness unto the truth. . . . *He was a burning and a shining light:* and ye were willing for a season to rejoice in his light" (John 5:33-35). Such words from the mouth of the Savior are, to say the least, a very high compliment to John.

When Jesus knew that John was in prison, he sent angels to minister to him (Matthew 4:11, I.V.). This also has a warmth and a flavor of compassion about it. Later, to the disciples of John who came to inquire of Jesus, the Master said, "*And blessed is John, and whosoever shall not be offended in me*" (Matthew 11:6, I.V.). Jesus then began to teach the multitudes about John:

> What went ye out into the wilderness to see? A reed shaken with the wind?
>
> But what went ye out for to see? A man clothed in soft raiment? behold, they that wear soft clothing are in kings' houses.
>
> But what went ye out for to see? A prophet? yea, I say unto you, and more than a prophet.
>
> For this is he, of whom it is written, Behold, I send my messenger before thy face, which shall prepare thy way before thee.
>
> Verily I say unto you, Among them that are born of women there hath not risen a greater than John the Baptist: notwithstanding he that is least in the kingdom of heaven is greater than he. [Matthew 11:7-11.]

It should be noted that Jesus identified John as the messenger spoken of by Malachi (verse 10, above; see Malachi 3:1). The further declaration that John was more than a prophet and that there had not arisen a greater than John is thought-provoking and has reference to John's unique privileges and opportunities. This matter was explained by the Prophet Joseph Smith:

> The question arose from the saying of Jesus — "Among those that are born of women there is not a greater prophet than John the Baptist; but he that is least in the kingdom of God is greater than he." How is it that John was considered one of the greatest prophets? His miracles could not have constituted his greatness.
>
> First. He was entrusted with a divine mission of preparing the way before the face of the Lord. Whoever had such a trust committed to him before or since? No man.
>
> Secondly. He was entrusted with the important mission, and it was

required at his hands, to baptize the Son of Man. Whoever had the honor of doing that? Whoever had so great a privilege and glory. Whoever led the Son of God into the waters of baptism, and had the privilege of beholding the Holy Ghost descend in the form of a dove, or rather in the *sign* of the dove, in witness of that administration? . . .

Thirdly. John, at that time, was the only legal administrator in the affairs of the kingdom there was then on the earth, and holding the keys of power. The Jews had to obey his instructions or be damned, by their own law; and Christ Himself fulfilled all righteousness in becoming obedient to the law which he had given to Moses on the mount, and thereby magnified it and made it honorable, instead of destroying it. The son of Zacharias wrested the keys, the kingdom, the power, the glory from the Jews, by the holy anointing and decree of heaven, and these three reasons constitute him the greatest prophet born of a woman. . . .

Second question: — How was the least in the kingdom of heaven greater than he?

In reply I asked — Whom did Jesus have reference to as being the least? Jesus was looked upon as having the least claim in God's kingdom, and [seemingly] was least entitled to their credulity as a prophet; as though He had said — "He that is considered the least among you is greater than John — that is I myself.[79]

Jesus went on to say that John had set up the kingdom of God, but that it was suffering from the violence of men who sought to take it by force. Yet the day would come, he said, when the violent would have no power. Furthermore, Jesus declared that John was "the Elias, who was for to come and prepare all things." The Inspired Version gives the clearer account, especially with regard to John's calling as the Elias to prepare all things:

King James Version	Inspired Version
Matt. 11:12 And from the days of John the Baptist until now the kingdom of heaven suffereth violence, and the violent take it by force.	Matt. 11:12 And from the days of John the Baptist until now, the kingdom of heaven suffereth violence, and the violent take it by force.
13 For all the prophets and the law prophesied until John.	13 *But the days will come, when the violent shall have no power;* for all the prophets and the law prophesied *that it should be thus* until John.
	14 *Yea, as many as have prophesied have foretold of these days.*

---

[79]*Teachings*, pp. 275-76.

14 And if ye will receive it, this is Elias, which was for to come.

15 And if ye will receive it, *verily, he was the* Elias, *who* was for to come *and prepare all things.*

When the Pharisees and lawyers "rejected the counsel of God against themselves" by not accepting John's baptism (Luke 7:30), Jesus lamented their unbelief. He spoke to them rather harshly, contrasting John's manner of life with his own and concluding with a declaration that no matter how the gospel was presented to that particular group they would reject it:

Whereunto then shall I liken the men of this generation? and to what are they like?

They are like unto children sitting in the marketplace, and calling one to another, and saying, We have piped unto you, and ye have not danced; we have mourned to you, and ye have not wept.

For John the Baptist came neither eating bread nor drinking wine; and ye say, He hath a devil.

The Son of man is come eating and drinking; and ye say, Behold a gluttonous man, and a winebibber, a friend of publicans and sinners! But wisdom is justified of all her children. [Luke 7:31-35.]

The passage is especially instructive for two reasons: first, it supports and compliments John; secondly, it relates that the Pharisees had accused John of having a devil — an allegation recorded nowhere else.

Later, when Jesus had driven the money changers from the temple, the chief priests and elders challenged him and asked of the source of his authority. This the Lord agreed to tell them if they would tell him of John's authority. The account is found in Matthew 21:23-27:

And when he was come into the temple, the chief priests and the elders of the people came unto him as he was teaching, and said, By what authority doest thou these things? and who gave thee this authority?

And Jesus answered and said unto them, I also will ask you one thing, which if ye tell me, I in like wise will tell you by what authority I do these things.

The baptism of John, whence was it? from heaven, or of men? And they reasoned with themselves, saying, If we shall say, From heaven; he will say unto us, Why did ye not then believe him?

But if we shall say, Of men; we fear the people; for all hold John as a prophet.

And they answered Jesus, and said, We cannot tell. And he said unto them, Neither tell I you by what authority I do these things.

Unwilling to concede that John had preached the gospel and performed baptisms by divine authority from heaven, the wily priests sought to avoid the issue by professing an inability to discern the situation. Their evasive answer was "We cannot tell." In the account recorded in the King James Version, Jesus did not at this point urge his own divinity upon them, but he did support and defend his servant John. He first related a short parable about two sons:

> But what think ye? A certain man had two sons; and he came to the first, and said, Son, go work to day in my vineyard.
> He answered and said, I will not: but afterward he repented, and went.
> And he came to the second, and said likewise. And he answered and said, I go, sir: and went not.
> Whether of them twain did the will of his father? They say unto him, The first. [Matthew 21:28-31.]

The first son in the parable was illustrative of the publicans and the harlots — sinners to be sure, but people who believed in the preaching of John and repented. The second son — he who professed obedience but did not obey — was representative of the Jewish religious leaders, that is, the very persons to whom Jesus was then speaking. Then Jesus spoke to them in defense of John:

> Verily I say unto you, That the publicans and the harlots go into the kingdom of God before you.
> For John came unto you in the way of righteousness, and ye believed him not: but the publicans and the harlots believed him: and ye, when ye had seen it, repented not afterward, that ye might believe him. [Matthew 21:31-32.]

The Inspired Version carries the situation a point further, so that Jesus not only bears witness of John's righteousness but also emphasizes John's testimony of him (Jesus). Unless they believed John, Jesus warned, John's preaching would condemn them on the day of judgment:

> For John came unto you in the way of righteousness, *and bore record of me*, and ye believed him not; but the publicans and harlots believed him; and ye, *afterward*, when ye had seen *me*, repented not, that ye might believe him.
> For he that believed not John concerning me, cannot believe me, except he first repent.
> And except ye repent, the preaching of John shall condemn you in the day of judgment. [Matthew 21:32-34, I.V.]

This is a much stronger affirmation than the account in the King James Version and is more consistent with the actual mission of John to bear witness of Jesus. It is also a stronger defense of John's work.

The news of John's death would have come as no surprise to Jesus, but the knowledge that it had been accomplished must have evoked some sympathy in the heart of the Master for his friend and fellow laborer whose mission was so closely allied to his own. Soon thereafter Jesus spoke about John the Baptist to Peter, James, and John on the holy mount, and said: "They knew him not, but have done unto him whatsoever they listed" (Matthew 17:12).

All in all, the scriptures tell of a warm and solid relationship between Jesus and John the Baptist. John was faithful unto death, and Jesus did not leave him comfortless. The Lord sustained and defended John as he does all of his faithful servants. About a year and a half after he was beheaded, John came forth and was with Christ in his resurrection (D&C 133:55).

Jesus' Final Comment about John

The final comment by Jesus about John the Baptist, as recorded in our present New Testament, was uttered during the Lord's forty-day ministry with his apostles after his resurrection. On this occasion Jesus told the Twelve to stay in Jerusalem and wait for the coming of the Holy Ghost, which had been promised them. "For," said he, "John truly baptized with water; but ye shall be baptized with the Holy Ghost not many days hence (Acts 1:5).

Thus the final affirmation of Jesus attesting to John's ministry. Later Peter made reference to this statement by Jesus when he was explaining to some critical brethren that the gospel is for the gentiles and not for the Jews only (Acts 11:2-4, 16-17).

As noted in chapter four, Peter had also referred earlier to the preaching of John (Acts 1:21-22); and at Antioch (in Pisidia) Paul preached to the Jews concerning John's ministry (Acts 13:23-25).

9
John and the Prophet Joseph Smith

From Moses to Jesus

John the Baptist is linked to three gospel dispensations. He was the very embodiment of the law of Moses, and functioned under the Aaronic order of priesthood. His life typified the purpose of the Law. Just as the law of Moses was a "schoolmaster to bring us unto Christ" (Galatians 3:24) and a preparation for the higher order of the gospel, so was John, as a man, the forerunner of the Messiah in person. He prepared the way, baptized the Messiah, and taught the people; and, having thus accomplished the purpose of his mission, faded into the background. John was the dominant figure in the closing of the Mosaic dispensation and a prominent figure in the opening of the dispensation of the meridian of time. As a holy angel, he has also ministered in building the dispensation of the fulness of times.

The Dispensation of the Fulness of Times

Approximately eighteen hundred years after his mortal life had been rudely terminated in the Machaerus dungeon, this same John, still holding the keys and priesthood of his ministry, descended from the skies as an angel of God in the glory of his resurrected body, in preparation for the Messiah's return and permanent reign upon the earth. Characteristic of his mission as a forerunner, he brought the priesthood of Aaron, which holds the keys of the preparatory gospel.

It was on Friday, the fifteenth day of May, 1829, that John ministered to Joseph Smith and Oliver Cowdery on the banks of the Susquehanna River near Harmony, Pennsylvania, and conferred on them the priesthood of Aaron. These were his words:

> Upon you my fellow servants, in the name of Messiah I confer the Priesthood of Aaron, which holds the keys of the ministering of angels, and of the gospel of repentance, and of baptism by immersion for the remission of sins; and this shall never be taken again from the earth, until the sons of Levi do offer again an offering unto the Lord in righteousness. [D&C 13.] [80]

Of this extraordinary event the Prophet Joseph wrote:

> The messenger who visited us on this occasion and conferred this Priesthood upon us, said that his name was John, the same that is called John the Baptist in the New Testament, and that he acted under the direction of Peter, James and John, who held the keys of the Priesthood of Melchizedek, which Priesthood, he said, would in due time be conferred on us. [Joseph Smith 2:72.]

At that time John also explained that the Aaronic Priesthood had not the power of laying on of hands for the gift of the Holy Ghost, but that this power would yet be conferred upon these two brethren (Joseph Smith 2:70).

Later, Oliver Cowdery wrote of the occasion in very glowing terms:

> There were days never to be forgotten. . . .
>
> . . . On a sudden, as from the midst of eternity, the voice of the Redeemer spake peace to us. While the veil was parted and the angel of God came down clothed with glory, and delivered the anxiously looked for message, and the keys of the Gospel of repentance. What joy! what wonder! what amazement! . . . Then his voice, though mild, pierced to the center, and his words, 'I am thy fellow-servant,' dispelled every fear. We listened, we gazed, we admired! 'Twas the voice of an angel, from glory, 'twas a message from the Most High! . . .
>
> . . . further think for a moment, what joy filled our hearts, . . . when we received under his hand the Holy Priesthood. . . .
>
> I shall not attempt to paint to you the feelings of this heart, nor the

---

[80] An account given by Oliver Cowdery reads a little differently, especially with reference to the sons of Levi. Instead of "and this priesthood shall never be taken again from the earth, *until* the sons of Levi do offer again an offering unto the Lord in righteousness," Cowdery reports John as saying, "and this authority . . . shall remain upon the earth, *that* the Sons of Levi *may yet* offer an offering unto the Lord in righteousness." (Published in *Times and Seasons*, 1 November 1840, p. 202, and quoted in a note at the end of Joseph Smith 2, in the Pearl of Great Price. My italics.)

majestic beauty and glory which surrounded us on this occasion; but you will believe me when I say, that earth, nor men, with the eloquence of time, cannot begin to clothe language in as interesting and sublime a manner as this holy personage.[81]

One can only imagine the thrill that came upon these two brethren when the hands of John were laid upon their heads, and they heard his voice speaking to them. Under John the Baptist's personal direction the first authorized baptisms of this dispensation were performed, with Joseph Smith first baptizing Oliver Cowdery, and then Oliver baptizing Joseph. Joseph then ordained Oliver to the Aaronic Priesthood, after which Oliver ordained Joseph to the same priesthood, according to the instructions given to them by the resurrected John (Joseph Smith 2:70-71). This was no ordinary event! Because of what took place on this occasion, May 15, 1829, shall forever be one of the most important days in the sacred history of the gospel among mankind.

A large bronze and granite monument depicting John the Baptist conferring the Aaronic Priesthood on Joseph and Oliver now stands on Temple Square in Salt Lake City.[82] The statues are 1¼ life size and show the two brethren kneeling while John stands with his right hand upon the head of Joseph and his left hand upon the head of Oliver. The world-renowned Dr. Avard Fairbanks was the sculptor. A bronze plaque on the base gives an account of the priesthood restoration. A similar structure also has been erected near the Susquehanna River in Pennsylvania, in the area where the ordination actually occurred.[83] Upon seeing these monuments, thousands of visitors to these two places will learn, or be reminded of, one of the world's great events.

---

[81]*Times and Seasons*, 1 November 1840, pp. 201-2, quoted in a note at the end of Joseph Smith 2.

[82]On October 5, 1956, an announcement was made by the First Presidency of the Church that a monument commemorating the restoration of the Aaronic Priesthood would be erected on Temple Square in Salt Lake City. The project was to be financed by voluntary contributions from Aaronic Priesthood members throughout the Church. In June 1957 a further announcement indicated that the project had been extended to include a second monument, to be placed near the Susquehanna River in Pennsylvania. In all, 65,000 persons donated money to the project. The structure in Salt Lake City was dedicated on October 10, 1958, by President David O. McKay. In the base of the monument, directly under the figure of John, a list of the names of the donors was placed in a copper box.

[83]The second monument was dedicated on June 18, 1960, under the direction of the Presiding Bishopric of the Church. The dedicatory prayer was offered by the then Presiding Bishop, Joseph L. Wirthlin.

Latter-day Aids to Understanding John the Baptist

The basic information about John the Baptist is contained in the New Testament. However, the revelations given to the Prophet Joseph Smith supply vital particulars that give us a more meaningful understanding of John. Each of the standard scriptural works produced in this dispensation contains considerable information about John the Baptist. An abundance of passages in the Book of Mormon, the Doctrine and Covenants, and the Pearl of Great Price present information about him. Likewise, many passages pertaining to John are revised and enlarged in Joseph Smith's Inspired Version of the Bible. And finally, John the Baptist was a frequent topic in the sermons and writings of the Prophet Joseph. The more prominent items about John that Joseph Smith discussed have been treated in this work. In summary, they are —

1. John's lineage (*Teachings*, p. 319);
2. the death of John's father (*Teachings*, p. 261);
3. John's ordination (D&C 84:28);
4. the limitations of John's mission (*Teachings*, pp. 335-36);
5. the legality of John's work (*Teachings*, pp. 318-19, 335-36);
6. John and the kingdom of God (*Teachings*, pp. 272-74);
7. baptisms by John (*Teachings*, pp. 272-74);
8. why it is said no prophet was greater than John (*Teachings*, pp. 275-76);
9. why the least in the kingdom is greater than John (*Teachings*, p. 276);
10. the ministering of angels to John (Matthew 4:11, I.V.);
11. John as an Elias (*Teachings*, pp. 335-36);
12. the record of John (D&C 93:6-18).

The information about John most adequately supplemented by latter-day revelation has to do with his credentials as a prophet. John's ordination, his own baptism, and his mission in the office and calling of Elias are all emphasized in the revelations given to Joseph Smith.

Just as the world has not understood any true prophet of God, so it does not understand John the Baptist. There is still much to be learned about John, even by members of the Church; yet students who believe in the revelations given to the Prophet Joseph Smith can have a greater appreciation for this "burning and a shining light" than can those who do not believe in the latter-day revelations.

John the Baptist and Joseph Smith

The following editorial, comparing John the Baptist and the

Prophet Joseph Smith as forerunners of the Savior, appeared in the *Church News* section of the *Salt Lake City Deseret News* for December 20, 1969, page 16. The comparison of the missions of these two great men, and the tribute paid to them, make an appropriate conclusion for this little work on John the Baptist.

The Forerunners

John the Baptist was sent to prepare the way for the Savior.

But why was this preparation needed? Were not the people of that day faithful to the law of Moses and were they not looking forward to their long-promised Messiah?

Would they not recognize the Lord by the plain descriptions given in Holy Writ? Why was a forerunner necessary?

The people of that day were anything but prepared for the Lord. Their leaders had become apostate. The elders, scribes and high priests had written their own creeds and as Jesus himself said, their traditions "transgressed the commandments of God." (Matt. 15.)

These apostate leaders were divided even among themselves. Some who denied the resurrection formed a sect known as Sadducees. Another sect or denomination which did accept the resurrection but were so apostate otherwise that they merited the most scathing denunciation of the Savior, were known as Pharisees.

Still another group was called Essenes. There were further schisms even among the elders and scribes. Under the law these professed believers were hopelessly divided, bitterly antagonistic and, far afield in their creeds and traditions.

The leaders in turn confused the people, most of whom hardly knew which way to turn. They were looking for the Messiah, they sought for light, but who could point the way?

Was the Messiah to come to a host of misguided, mistaught unbelievers, blinded by the long-standing traditions of men?

Or was there a way to bring together a humble, teachable, even though small group, who would accept Him gladly, and from among whom He could choose His own true ministers to carry on His work when He was no longer on earth?

He himself was to minister for only a short three years. It would be so helpful if the way were prepared in advance.

So John was sent. He was taught and trained and ordained from above. He mingled with none of the arrogant as he grew up. He was untouched and unspoiled by their false creeds and traditions. He lived apart from them all — in the wilderness.

As he began his ministry, he called everyone to repentance, to believe the Gospel, and prepare for the Messiah whose shoe latches he said he was not worthy to unloose. The Messiah would baptize with fire and with the Holy Ghost.

After John had prepared a group of believers, Jesus came to him, seeking baptism. John recognized Him as the Messiah and said to his own followers: "Behold the Lamb of God," and John's disciples accepted Jesus on John's own word.

Through the work of the Baptist, Jesus now had a ready-made nucleus upon which He could build. From among these humble believers came some of Christ's most faithful followers.

Then as John explained, his own mission began to diminish but Christ's increased. So John prepared the way for the first coming.

But Jesus is to come again. His second appearance will be in great contrast to His first. At first He came humbly. Next time He will come in glory. So spectacular will be this appearance that great signs in the heavens will announce it, the heavenly hosts will be with Him, and all mankind will see it together.

But is there need of a preparatory work in anticipation of such a magnificent event? Or does the world not need it?

Does man-made tradition obscure the truth now as it did when John was but a voice crying in the wilderness?

All must agree that the world is just as divided, just as corrupt, as it was in the days of John. As a forerunner was needed for Christ's first appearance, so one is urgently required for His second coming.

And as the glorious second advent will tremendously transcend His humble first appearance, so the preparatory work must be more extensive than that which John did. This the scriptures foretold:

It will include the gathering of Israel and provide a restitution of all things whatsoever God has spoken from the beginning of the world.

A new volume of scripture is to come forth, called by Isaiah a marvelous work and a wonder. The house of the Lord must be established in the tops of the mountains. And the Gospel of the kingdom shall be preached to all nations and then shall the end come.

But who can direct all this preparatory work?

Only a modern divinely appointed forerunner!

And has he come? He has. And what is his name? Joseph Smith, the Mormon Prophet!

As John the Baptist prepared the way for the Lord's first coming, so Joseph Smith, in a similar role, is the forerunner of latter days. . . .[84]

---

[84]"The Forerunners," courtesy of *Church News, Deseret News.*

Bibliography

Books

Clark, J. Reuben, Jr. *Our Lord of the Gospels.* Salt Lake City: Deseret Book Company, 1954.

Farrar, Frederic W. *The Life of Christ.* Portland: Fountain Publications, 1960.

Gale, Nahum. *John the Baptist; or, The Prophet of the Highest.* Boston: American Tract Society, n.d.

Geikie, Cunningham. *The Life and Words of Christ.* 2 vols. New York: D. Appleton and Company, 1879.

Godet, Frederic. *Commentary on the Gospel of John.* 2 vols. New York: Funk and Wagnalls, Publishers, 1886.

Hastings, James, ed. *Dictionary of the Bible.* New York: Charles Scribner's Sons, 1963.

James, Montague Rhodes, trans. *The Apocryphal New Testament.* Oxford: The Clarendon Press, 1953.

Jameson, Anna Brownell. *The History of Our Lord as Exemplified in Works of Art.* London: Longman, Green, Longman, Roberts, & Green, 1865.

Josephus, Flavius. *Antiquities of the Jews.* In *The Complete Works of Flavius Josephus.* Translated by William Whiston. New York: Holt, Rinehart and Winston, Inc., n.d. but recent.

McConkie, Bruce R. *Doctrinal New Testament Commentary.* 2 vols. Salt Lake City: Bookcraft, 1965.

Palmer, Lee A. *Aaronic Priesthood Through the Centuries*. Salt Lake City: Deseret Book Company, 1964.

Ricciotti, Giuseppe. *The Life of Christ*. Milwaukee: The Bruce Publishing Company, 1947.

Robertson, Archibald T. *John the Loyal*. New York: Charles Scribner's Sons, 1911.

Scobie, Charles H. H. *John the Baptist*. Philadelphia: Fortress Press, 1964.

Smith, Joseph Fielding, comp. *Teachings of the Prophet Joseph Smith*. Salt Lake City: Deseret Book Company, 1938.

————. *Answers to Gospel Questions*. 5 vols. Salt Lake City: Deseret Book Company, 1957-66.

Steinmann, Jean. *Saint John the Baptist and the Desert Tradition*. Translated by Michael Boyes. New York: Harper and Brothers [1958].

Talmage, James E. *Jesus the Christ*. Salt Lake City: Deseret Book Company, 1956.

Scriptures

The Holy Bible. King James Version.

The Holy Bible. The New Catholic Confraternity Edition. New York: Catholic Book Publishing Co., 1962. Translated from the Latin Vulgate.

The Holy Scriptures. Inspired Revision by Joseph Smith, Jr. 2d ed. rev. Independence, Mo.: Reorganized Church of Jesus Christ of Latter Day Saints, 1944.

The New American Bible. Translated from the original languages by members of the Catholic Biblical Association of America. Sponsored and published by the Bishops' Committee of the Confraternity of Christian Doctrine, Washington, D. C. New York: Benziger, Inc., 1970.

The New English Bible: New Testament. Oxford University Press and Cambridge University Press, 1961.

The New Testament, American Standard Version. Cincinnati: Standard Publishing, 1901.

Das Neue Testament. From a translation by Martin Luther. Printed in Stuttgart, Germany, by the Wittenburg Bible House, 1964.

The Four Gospels According to the Eastern Version. Translated from the Aramaic by George M. Lamsa. Philadelphia: A. J. Holman Company, 1933.

The Book of Mormon.

The Doctrine and Covenants.

The Pearl of Great Price.

Periodicals

Barrett, C. K. "The Lamb of God," *New Testament Studies,* 1:210-18 (1954-55).

Brownlee, William H. "A Comparison of the Covenanters of the Dead Sea Scrolls with Pre-Christian Jewish Sects." *The Biblical Archaeologist,* 13:50-72 (1950).

————. "John the Baptist in the New Light of Ancient Scrolls." *Interpretation,* 9:71-90 (1955).

"The Forerunners." *Church News* (weekly section of *Salt Lake City Deseret News*), 20 December 1969, p. 16.

Grobel, Kendrick. "He That Cometh After Me." *Journal of Biblical Literature,* 60:397-401 (1941).

Times and Seasons, vol. 2, no. 1 (1 November 1840), pp. 201-2.

Scripture Index

119

Subject Index

Aaron
  John the Baptist a literal
    descendant of, 17-18
  origin of priesthood of, 11-13
Aaronic Priesthood
  conferred on Joseph Smith and
    Oliver Cowdery by John the
    Baptist, 22 n
  continued among house of Aaron
    until John the Baptist, 22-23
  has not power to confer Holy
    Ghost, 108
  held by Zacharias, 22
  holds keys of ministering of angels,
    108
  keys of, held by John the Baptist,
    22, 30, 52, 107
  origin of, 11-13
  specific lineage of, 17
Abraham
  covenant of, 57
  John the Baptist understood
    covenant of, 56-57
  premortal appointment of, 8
Aenon, near Salim
  John the Baptist at, 39, 85-86
  location of, a matter of question, 39,
    85-86

Ahab
  Herod likened to, 97
Angels
  Aaronic Priesthood holds keys to
    ministering of, 108
  John the Baptist received visitation
    of, during his formative years, 30
  ministered to John the Baptist in
    prison, 91-92, 110
Aretas
  daughter of, married to Herod
    Antipas, 87, 96
  defeated Herod Antipas in battle, 87,
    96-97
  king of Arabia, 87
  mentioned by Josephus, 87
  mentioned by Paul, 87 n

Baptism by water
  administered to Jesus by John the
    Baptist, 35
  administered under Aaronic
    Priesthood, 108
  given to multitudes by John the
    Baptist, 34
  misunderstanding of, by twelve
    disciples at Ephesus, 44, 76-78
  validity of John the Baptist's, 76-78

121

122

important in history and doctrine of
   The Church of Jesus Christ of
   Latter-day Saints, 3, 107, 109
imprisonment of, 90-91
length of ministry of, 41-42
likened to Elijah, 98-105
manner of dress of, 26
martyr for the gospel's sake, 97-98
mission of, foretold in prophecy, 4-6
no miracles performed by, 96, 100
ordination of, 21-23 @ 8 days old
popularity of, with multitudes, 103
possible Samaritan ministry of,
   85-86
possible torture of, 90-91
praised by Jesus, 3, 101
probable betrayal of, by Pharisees,
   43, 88
resurrection of, 98, 105
saw sign of dove, 35, 37, 60-65
semi-apostolic calling of, 64
sent disciples to Jesus, 91-93
special kind of man, 9-10
strength of character of, 8, 9-10, 40-
   41, 98
taught by revelation, 28-30, 64
taught Herod's servants, 95
testified of divinity of Jesus Christ,
   62, 74
testimony of, will condemn Jews on
   day of judgment, 104-5
threefold testimony of, 100
three-phase ministry of, 37
time of ministry clarified by
   Inspired Version of Bible, 31-34
voice of the Father heard by, 35, 61,
   64-65
written record by, 79-83
John the Beloved
   disciple of John the Baptist, 43-44, 81
   record of John the Baptist quoted by,
      80
   writings of, show great familiarity
      with ministry of John the Baptist, 81
Kingdom of God
   explanation of, 49-51
   rested with John the Baptist for a
      time, 52

Law of Moses
   explained by Book of Mormon, 12-13
   John the Baptist the very
      embodiment of, 107

obeyed by John the Baptist, 18, 28
origin of, 10-13
Luther, Martin
   quoted on greatness of John the
      Baptist, 45, 45 n

Machaerus
   archaeological remains of, 90 n
   identified by Josephus, 90
   John beheaded in, 94
   John imprisoned in, 90
   located near eastern shore of Dead
      Sea, 90, 93
   not mentioned by name in Bible, 90
McConkie, Bruce R.
   quoted on John the Baptist at Mount
      of Transfiguration, 72
   quoted on ordination of John the
      Baptist, 22
   quoted on record of John the Baptist,
      81
Melchizedek Priesthood
   keys of, held by Peter, James, and
      John, 108
Moses. See also Law of Moses
   on Mount of Transfiguration, 72
Mount of Transfiguration
   John the Baptist at, 72

Noah. See Gabriel

Ordination
   of John the Baptist, 21-23
   of Joseph Smith and Oliver Cowdery,
      108-9.

Paul
   Aretas mentioned by, 87 n
   found so-called disciples of John the
      Baptist at Ephesus, 44, 76-77
   John the Baptist spoken of by, 105
Peter
   spoke of John the Baptist, 38, 105
Pharisees
   accused John the Baptist of having a
      devil, 103
   came to see John the Baptist baptize,
      55-56
   denied validity of John the Baptist's
      baptism, 88
   denounced by John the Baptist, 34,
      55-57
   inquired about John the Baptist's

124